500

Tips

for

Teachers

Second Edition

**SALLY BROWN, CAROLYN EARLAM
AND PHIL RACE**

**KOGAN
PAGE**

First published in 1994
Second edition 1998
Reprinted 1999

Kogan Page Limited
120 Pentonville Road
London N1 9JN, UK
and
Stylus Publishing Inc.
22883 Quicksilver Drive
Sterling, VA 20166, USA

British Library Cataloguing in Publication Data

A CIP record for this book is available from the British Library.

ISBN 0 7494 2835 X

Typeset by Jo Brereton, Primary Focus, Haslington, Cheshire
Printed and bound in the UK, Biddles Ltd, Guildford and Kings Lynn

Contents

Our aims in this book

This book is designed to be a useful compendium of sound and practical ideas to help classroom teachers in secondary schools to do the job to the best of their ability, particularly but not exclusively those who are new to the profession. It is primarily aimed at secondary school teachers who are extremely busy simply keeping up with their work, and whose time for reading the literature on teaching and learning is limited, but who may welcome ready-to-use practical suggestions on a wide range of their everyday activities.

There were over 500 tips in the first edition of this book. In this the second edition, there are now nearly 700! We have strengthened the first section by adding a set of tips on 'Strategies for raising achievement' in line with current thinking about the need to enable all pupils to achieve their full potential. A companion volume to this book is *500 Tips for School Improvement* (Helen Horne and Sally Brown) which takes these issues further. The most significant addition in this edition is an extensive final chapter, comprising 13 new sets of suggestions addressing the well-identified need to ensure that information and communications technologies are incorporated appropriately into all areas of the curriculum. The 'National Grid for Learning' in the UK will provide exciting opportunities to enable widest possible access to the technologies which will underpin every aspect of our lives in the future.

Although those who work with younger children may find elements of this book helpful, *500 Tips for Primary Teachers* in the same format is likely to contain suggestions that are even more relevant to them. While many of the tips are also transferable to further and higher education, other books in this series such as *500 Tips for Further and Continuing Education Lecturers* and *500 Tips for Tutors* are more closely focused on their respective areas of the profession.

Please don't read this book cover to cover!

This book is designed to be dipped into, with readers selecting those areas that are of most interest to them. We have assembled 65 sets of tips, each set intended to be relatively complete in itself. We have grouped the sets under seven main headings, although sometimes these divisions have been rather arbitrary, with some sets being perfectly capable of being sited in two or more categories. However, as this is a book for grazing on rather than devouring whole, we don't consider that problematic. We hope, however, that the contents pages and chapter titles will help you to find quickly those parts of the book that could be of most immediate value to you.

This book does not aim to cover everything!

Obviously a book of hints and tips is meant to support, and not replace, the broad learning achieved by teachers on properly accredited training programmes. This book is designed to be a handy supplement to such programmes. Furthermore, we know from our own work that many of the most valuable and important lessons are learned only by practice, having a go at things, and trial and error, rather than reading what has already been written about them, or hearing experienced people tell us about them. Experienced teachers are bound to have learned innumerable wrinkles of their own from their practice, but we hope that they will find useful food for thought in this book amidst all sorts of suggestions that they have already developed for themselves. Newly qualified teachers, however, we hope will find this book a useful companion to them in their first year or two of practice, helping them to handle each new situation as they meet it.

Acknowledgements

Thanks are due to everyone who gave us most constructive advice and criticism at the pilot stage of this book, especially: Tom Carr, Diana Le Cornu, Myles Easterby, Mary Evans, Diane Green, Andrea Heron, Helen Horne, Rob Merville and Geoff Myers.

Sally Brown: *Head of Quality Enhancement, University of Northumbria at Newcastle.*
Carolyn Earlam: *Inspector for Art and Design, Durham County Council Education Department.*
Phil Race: *Programme Director: University of Durham Certificate in Teaching in Higher Education.*

May 1998

Chapter 1 Techniques for effective teaching and classroom management

This section contains some advice on some basic techniques of teaching, particularly on interaction with pupils. This is perhaps one of the most difficult areas on which to give advice, because the way we work with children tends to be a very personal thing. Techniques that work with one teacher can sometimes prove to be completely useless to another, and it is really important to develop your own style, with which you feel comfortable. People tend to talk about 'natural authority' as though it were something that one is either born with or not, but in reality everyone has good days and bad days. The principal advantages of being an experienced teacher include that you have learned not to take unpleasant experience too seriously and you can learn from mistakes. In this chapter, we aim to share some very practical tips on teaching techniques. If you have already passed the stage of needing such suggestions, please pass on to later chapters of the book.

1

Meeting a class for the first time

There is no second chance to make a good first impression! First impressions are crucial in any work with people and none more so than with new pupils. The old adage 'don't smile until Christmas' held a grain of truth – it's always easier to loosen up later than it is to start to lay down the law once your class has decided you're soft!

1   **Don't forget to introduce yourself** – and spell your name out on the blackboard if necessary. Pupils in Primary School usually know their teachers quite well, and see the same teachers for a greater proportion of the time than in secondary education. It can be quite stressful for pupils to start a new school, or a new year, in which they may encounter 20 new teachers in the space of a week.

2   **State clearly what you expect of your pupils** – what they can and cannot do in the classroom. Establish a few simple rules of behaviour and always stick to them. You may also wish to invite from pupils their own suggestions for additional groundrules.

3   **Learn your pupils' names as quickly as you can** – any instruction is much more effective if directed to an individual. Your work will also be more effective if you never forget that your class is made up of individuals, and know them as such.

4   **Help pupils to learn each others' names** if they don't know them already. One way of doing this is to form them into a large circle, and ask each pupil to say (for example) 'my name is Cheryl, and this is my friend Mark, and this is Clive, and ...' seeing who can say the most names. This helps you learn their names too!

5   **Help pupils to get to know each other** (at the same time helping you to get to know them). For example, conduct a class round along the lines of 'My name is Jean, my favourite thing in the world is pizza, and my pet hate is spiders'.

6   **Show your pupils where they're heading.** Give your pupils a clear idea of what they will be doing in the next few weeks and why they are doing it. Help them to see how your work with them fits in with the syllabus, National Curriculum programmes of study and so on.

7   **Make sure your pupils know how they will be assessed.** Which pieces of work are more important for assessment, which areas are revision of material they have already covered? Emphasize the need for them to look after their own work and take responsibility for their own progress, especially where there is continuous assessment.

8   Use the first lessons to **find out what pupils already know** about the subject and build on this in your planning. You could make this into a quiz or get them to write something which is personal to them which will help you get to know them.

9   **Explain which resources are available for pupils to use;** which they can access themselves and which resources are to be obtained from the teacher, or in the library or resource centre. Encourage pupils to take responsibility for the resources in their classroom, for example keeping an eye on the numbers of rulers, rubbers, and so on, ensuring that the stock lasts all year.

10   **React firmly if any of your rules of behaviour are transgressed.** This is especially important in the first few weeks. Show the class that you notice everything that is going on and are not willing to ignore anything. Name the pupil who has done something you don't like, but be aware of individual personalities and notice if what you say is having an extreme effect on anyone. You may need to tread carefully with pupils who feel insecure or nervous. Don't be drawn into arguments; when you know pupils better you can be more flexible.

2

Gaining attention and settling a class down

Nice as it would be if all pupils were sitting quietly, ready to learn, and attentive at all times, this is not the nature of the young of the human species! Here are some tips to overcome human nature – but remember that different things work for different people, so find your own styles.

1   **Try doing nothing first.** Stand there, very still, absolutely quiet. The pupils closest will notice, and the word will gradually spread. Give it a moment or two before you decide that another tactic is needed!

2   **Don't shout (yet)!** If all is not quiet, avoid the instinct to shout 'be quiet' at the top of your voice! Start a quiet conversation with two or three pupils who already look ready to listen to you.

3   **Take advantage of human curiosity.** It sometimes pays to whisper! Human nature includes not wishing to miss anything. Whisper to those closest to you, and many of the rest will stop talking and listen.

4   **Drop a non-attender in it!** Ask a question to those who are already listening, but end with the name of someone you know has not been paying attention. Watch as all eyes turn to this pupil, the effect of someone being found out by their peers not to have been listening.

5   **Have ways of making pupils listen.** Start with something that needs careful listening – for example a tape-recording or video played back quite quietly.

6   **People love praise.** Praise those who are paying attention, particularly if they don't normally, rather than grumbling at those pupils who are not yet paying attention.

7   **Begin with a task.** Start a session with something for pupils to do. Have printed instructions on handout materials, or write them on the blackboard in advance.

8   **Select some targets.** Pick on some 'known' live-wires in the class by name, giving them particular tasks to do at the start of a lesson, as leaders of groups of pupils.

9   **Don't take chaos as a personal affront.** Don't regard initial chaos as disrespect to you. Regard it as human nature, and natural until something interesting comes up.

10   **Few want to be left out of some fun!** If you can do this (we're not good at it!) start a lesson by very quietly saying something really amusing to those who have already 'settled down'. The rest will soon become eager to be included in this.

3

Coping with interruptions

'If only I could just get on with my teaching!'– how often have we thought this. When we're interrupted, it's natural to feel emotions including anger and frustration. However, at these times, all eyes tend to be on us – not least to see how we react. The following suggestions may help you deal with interruptions with dignity.

1   **Accept that you are in fact being interrupted.** Trying to carry on as though the source of the interruption was unnoticed tends to do more harm than good, as most pupils will probably be concentrating on the interruption, and how you react, rather than on what you had been saying or doing just before the event.

2   **Keep track of where you were.** Make a mental note of exactly what you were doing just before an interruption, so that when you have dealt with it, you can pick up the threads without having to say 'now, where was I?' Also, check whether there are connections between things you do and the probability of interruptions.

3   **Accept that some interruptions will be important and necessary.** When this is so, make sure that anyone responsible for the interruption is not criticized or made to feel embarrassed.

4   **Be patient with colleagues.** Be particularly careful when interrupted by a colleague or other member of staff. Even if the interruption is unwelcome and unnecessary, it is best to have a quiet word with the person concerned later, rather than let any frustration be noticed by your pupils.

5   **Turn interruptions into positive learning experiences.** When possible, draw useful learning points from interruptions by pupils. The more they feel that their interruptions are taken notice of, the more likely they are to avoid making unnecessary ones.

6   **Keep individual feelings for individuals.** When a particular pupil is making too many interruptions, try to have a private word later, rather than a public show of annoyance.

7   **Have something to do ready for anyone who interrupts.** Have a list of relevant questions about the topic of the day, so that anyone who interrupts can be put on the spot if necessary with a question to answer. This can work well at discouraging interruptions!

8   **Watch your distance.** Move up close to anyone who has made an unwelcome interruption. Pupils are much less brave when you're standing over them than when you're at the other end of the room.

9   **Look for the causes of interruptions.** If there are frequent interruptions, it could be that pupils are tired of listening, and need to be given something definite to get on with. Avoid the 'I've started, so I'll finish' approach.

10 **Learn from colleagues.** When you have the chance, observe how colleagues cope with interruptions. The more techniques you have at your disposal, the more versatile your approach becomes.

4

Learning names

You will know yourself how irritating it is when people forget your own name. Calling someone by name makes any message you wish to communicate all the stronger and more personal. However, we often seem to have a whole bunch of new names to tackle at once: the following suggestions may help you with this task. There will always be some names that are very hard to remember, but it's worth making the effort: you may be the only person who does learn such names.

1   **Let pupils decide their names!** Ask your pupils to tell you the version of their name they wish to be known by and attempt to call them by it unless it is too daft for you to cope with. Michael might hate being called Mick, but Salim might prefer Sal.

2   **Be careful with nicknames.** Be cautious about using nicknames that seem innocuous enough to us, but cause the class to fall about hysterically every time you use it. It may well be that you are unwittingly being drawn into using an unknown (to you) vulgar expression!

3   **Address questions to named pupils.** To help you to get to know some names, choose people from the class list to answer (easy) questions and bit by bit memorize the respondents' names.

4   **Make a map of the names.** Use a seating plan to note names of pupils next to where they are sitting and try to encourage them to sit there for the first few lessons until you are more familiar with the class.

5   **Once you've got them, use them.** Once you know some names, use them every time you speak to those pupils (without letting them feel they are being picked on!).

6   **Make names visual.** Some pupils will be happy to wear name labels for the first few days of a session, or you could use folded cardboard name labels on the desk: remember to get them to write their names in really large letters.

7   **One step at a time!** Concentrate on first names for the first part of the school year, and pick up the surnames as you go on.

8   **Take care with the repetitions.** Find out any pupils who share a first name and learn these first, once you have learned the three Matthews, two Traceys and four Alis you have made a good start!

9   **Make sure you have their names right.** Check you are using the correct names for pupils and encourage them to correct you if you get them wrong. Also check out how to pronounce unfamiliar names. It's dreadful to find out at the end of the year that you have been getting one wrong from the beginning.

10 **Be persistent.** Don't expect to learn all the names all at once: build up gradually over the weeks. Don't be too hard on yourself if you never master all of the names, especially if you teach lots of different groups. But do your best: pupils do tend to be critical of teachers who don't make an effort to learn names.

5

Avoiding disruption in your class

This is an area a great deal easier to write about than to follow through – but we all keep battling against the unpredictability of the human factor!

1   **Establish a few, clear rules for behaviour in your class.** If possible involve the pupils in the development of these rules. The more ownership you can allow them to feel regarding the rules, the more likely they are to at least try to follow them.

2   **Reward good behaviour immediately with positive feedback** – a smile or a few words of praise or encouragement. Try also to ensure that you are quick to reward the good behaviour of any pupils who are often guilty of bad behaviour – they may really respond to some positive feedback.

3   **Deal with any misdemeanours before they become major incidents.** Often, it is best to deal with minor incidents as privately as you can. Public confrontations arouse too much interest!

4   **Establish what the sanctions will be for transgressing the rules.** Ensure that such sanctions are reasonable and practicable.

5   **Avoid unreasonable expectations of pupils – but don't demean them either.** Ensure that the level of the work you set is suitable for all the individuals within the group, and that pupils experiencing difficulties have manageable targets. Direct the emphasis of your comments towards the work or lack of it. This involves getting to know what each pupil is capable of, and setting realistic targets.

6   **Look for signals.** Be adaptable – change the pace or content of a lesson as soon as you realize it is not working well. Changing approach on the basis of feedback you receive is a strength, not a weakness!

7   **If a particular pupil is causing problems**, immediately remove this pupil to another part of the room. This is a way of demonstrating that you have observed the problem, and also provides such a pupil with the opportunity to start afresh.

8   **Provide 'cooling-off' time.** If you – or a pupil – lose your temper, try to allow a few minutes for you both to calm down: take the pupil involved out from the room for a short while. It can pave the way towards progress to say something along the lines 'I'm sorry this happened. How can we make sure that this sort of thing doesn't happen again?'

9   **Investigate the causes of bad behaviour.** Talk to a pupil who has caused problems away from the class, on a one to one basis and try to find out the reasons for misbehaviour. Sometimes, the reasons (once known) will be very understandable and forgivable.

10   **Have ready something interesting to give the class to do.** This can be invaluable when you need time to calm down yourself, or when you need to have those few quiet words outside the door with an individual pupil who has been causing problems. Prepare a verbal quiz or game for the last ten minutes, either as a reward for work well done, or because you have finished a useful activity and need a change.

6

Using blackboards

There's a blackboard or whiteboard in most teaching rooms. We sometimes feel so close to this in our professional lives that the term 'life at the chalkface' is in common use! How we use the most straightforward of our visual aids can make a big difference to how much our pupils learn.

1 **How visible are your etchings?** Check that the size of your writing is such that the pupils who are furthest away from the board can read what you put on the board.

2 **Aim for the top!** Ensure that you make good use of the upper half of the board, and only use the rest of the board if you know that pupils at the back aren't screened from viewing by those closer to the board.

3 **Show your agenda.** Use the board to write questions that you will be discussing, so pupils can continue to see the questions as you develop with them the answers.

4 **If you are left-handed, you may find writing on the blackboard difficult.** This is not your ineptitude, but because you are pushing the chalk. It has taken some teachers years of distress to discover this! Left-handed chalk-users (e.g. PR) sometimes find that standing a little more to the right than usual, and pulling the chalk that bit more, helps improve the situation.

5 **Be heard as well as seen.** Don't talk to the class while you're writing on the board with your back to your pupils. When possible, arrange the room so that you can maintain eye-contact with most of your pupils even while you're writing on the board.

6 **Be prepared!** Whenever you have the chance, prepare a blackboard in advance for a class, so that pupils can see an outline of the things you're going to talk about in the forthcoming lesson straightaway.

7   **Get your pupils' words on the blackboard.** Whenever you can, use the blackboard to write up things that pupils tell you in answer to your questions, so that they can see their thinking being valued and acknowledged by you. When pupils see you write up *their* words, their ownership of what is going on is increased, and their attention may improve.

8   **Let pupils have a turn with the chalk.** Make the blackboard 'everyone's' territory. Ask pupils to write things on it, for example, questions they want to ask, ideas they want to discuss, and interesting things they want to talk about.

9   **Use the blackboard as a classroom resource.** Give groups of pupils 'blackboard tasks', for example when starting a new topic, ask groups to compose and write up 'ten questions we want to know about it'.

10 **Be careful with the rubber!** Before you erase comments suggested or written by pupils, give a further acknowledgement of the value of these comments.

7

Organizing practical lessons

Practical lessons can so easily turn into chaos if not well organized, however well planned the content is. Don't try anything new with a class unless you have done it yourself in advance and know it works – and save time in demonstrating by showing 'the one you made earlier'.

1   **Put safety first.** There is a wide range of safety legislation, particularly covering equipment and materials that are potentially hazardous. If your work involves dangerous things, take every opportunity to get yourself some relevant safety training. If something were to go wrong, the buck could rest with you.

2   **Check through the materials you require before the lesson starts.** Ensure they are prepared for use. You can waste many minutes (seems like hours) trying to unscrew a jar whilst the class gets bored and runs riot.

3   **Assemble your materials in labelled boxes or trays.** This is well worth doing when it is a lesson you will repeat, and can save you much time organizing the same materials in future.

4   **Engage the help of the class.** Let pupils help to distribute materials and equipment, and in cleaning up at the end of the session. It will save you time and help pupils learn how to look after resources. Allow plenty of time for clearing up; it may take much longer than you think in the early stages.

5   **Make sure you have enough materials for everyone.** Or at least have enough for pupils to work in pairs. When pupils are not fully involved themselves, they tend to experiment in ways of which you would not approve!

6   **Give short, clear instructions about the task required.** Ask questions of those pupils who seem not to be concentrating to ensure that they have understood. Their repetition of the requirements of the task will reinforce the instructions to the others.

7   **Make demonstrations snappy.** When you are demonstrating an activity or an experiment it is easy to take so long explaining the 'right' way of doing something that pupils who are itching to try it themselves at first become turned off.

8   **Establish firm rules of behaviour.** Disruption or silliness may prove not only counter-productive to learning, but can turn out to be very dangerous, for example if your class is working with chemicals or electrical equipment.

9   **Avoid the necessity for pupils to queue for your advice or opinion.** Teach pupils to be self-reliant and resourceful, and to help each other if they can't do something or find something.

10   **Bring the class back together at intervals.** Talk to the whole class during activities. Everyone may be working at a different rate, and some pupils will need this structure to avoid being left behind.

11   **Evaluate the activity.** Make time towards the end of a practical lesson for some kind of evaluation. You may not have had time to get round to every individual, and in this way you can ensure that all pupils receive some feedback.

8

Doing yard/bus/break duties painlessly

'Oh no, not all this as well?' you may have exclaimed, when first you discovered that you were expected to do such duties! Sadly, being a teacher is not just about teaching. We also need to help keep the school going during the times when we're not teaching. The following suggestions may help you tackle this with equanimity!

1   **Get a whistle!** Don't worry that they are a bit old-fashioned. They can help you gain attention in noisy circumstances – as long as you don't over-use them.

2   **Make sure you know the rules.** Know what is allowed and what is not. Try to get a thorough briefing from an experienced colleague who can show you the ropes.

3   **Be seen, and heard!** Should you need to enter the toilets or go behind the bike shed, announce your presence loudly. You are less likely to have unpleasant surprises that way!

4   **Wrap up warm on cold days – and be prepared for rain!** Such duties are made more miserable than ever if you are unsuitably dressed. If you can get a hot drink as well, so much the better.

5   **Try pairing up with a colleague.** If your duties turn out to be a hard chore for you, you can either keep each other company or cover each other for short periods so that you each get some sort of break. A 20-minute yard-duty can feel a lot longer than two 10-minute half-duties. If possible, shadow a colleague on the relevant duty before your actual turn comes up, so that you know what may be expected of you before you tackle it on your own.

6   **Pave the way.** Try to be especially well-prepared in advance if you know you will be teaching immediately after a duty. This can ensure that you are not too flustered at the start of the ensuing lesson. Give the class something to do that really keeps them busy while you get your breath back!

7   **Have contingency plans for what to do if things go wrong.** Check out what the school policy is on minor accidents or incidents. With younger pupils, it may be useful to have readily available supplies of antiseptic wipes and plasters.

8   **Keep your eyes peeled!** It isn't possible to have your eyes everywhere, but you can often prevent trouble by stepping in before it happens. The price of peace is eternal vigilance!

9   **If fights break out, think carefully about your interventions.** You can restrain pupils using 'reasonable force' where the safety of a pupil or a colleague is threatened, but these conditions may not be easy to interpret. Under no circumstances should you ever strike a pupil.

10   **Use such duties as occasions when you can build up good relations with pupils outside the classroom.** Be careful, however, not to put yourself at risk of seeming to have favourites, or of giving excessively exceptional attention to particular individual pupils.

9

Ensuring equality of opportunity within your teaching

The suggestions in this section relate to anti-oppressive practice in all areas, including race, gender, sexuality, age and disability. It is increasingly necessary in our society to tackle inequality head-on, and the sooner the better. The following suggestions should help you treat all pupils (and colleagues) equally, and help them to value equality.

1   **Check that you are behaving in the same way towards all pupils.** Check that you are not treating pupils, whatever their background, differently in lessons, when you ask questions or let pupils give comments.

2   **Arrange that group work is done in mixed-gender groups.** At certain ages pupils' natural tendency is to sit in same-gender groupings, and you may have to intervene in natural seating arrangements. Don't work from gender lists when arranging groups, use a more random characteristic such as birth dates or colour of hair.

3   **Get your tongue round *all* your pupils' names!** Make an effort to be able to pronounce the names of pupils with names unfamiliar to you, without any hesitation or insecurity. Allow them to keep telling you whether you've got their names right or not yet.

4   **Avoid discriminatory type-casting.** In designing class exercises, case-studies or scenarios, ensure that you are not type-casting roles according to race, gender, sexuality, age or disability. Also, avoid the tendency to ask only boys to help to move furniture, lift boxes, open jars and bottles, or to ask only girls to tidy up or clean benches.

5   **Help colleagues to avoid discrimination.** Be sensitive to instances where colleagues violate equal opportunities principles, and bring such occasions to their notice. Don't expect an easy ride when chastening some colleagues on their practice in this respect, but continue to give them the chance to be reminded that it is an important issue.

6   **Watch your sense of humour!** It is dangerously easy to attempt to say something amusing, when in fact the fun is at someone's expense. Do not use jokes or anecdotes which could be interpreted as oppressive to any group.

7   **Raise pupils' awareness of equality issues.** Encourage pupils to confront issues of inequality objectively, and help them to work out practical and viable solutions to problems involving equal opportunity.

8   **Be on the lookout for pupils who may be affected by inequality.** Seek feedback from all pupils to probe any feelings they may have regarding being treated unequally in any respect.

9   **Reflect equality in your own work.** Proactively seek to work collaboratively with colleagues of different race, gender, sexuality, age and ability, whenever the opportunity arises.

10   **Don't let pupils get away with bias.** Censure any pupils who display inappropriate bias in things they say or write, and help them towards attitudes which enable them to demonstrate equality values.

10

Strategies for raising achievement

The focus of teaching and learning is centrally concerned with adding value to student achievement, through a variety of techniques which enhance pupils' performance across the curriculum. The following suggestions are designed to help you to do so strategically.

1   **Plan and prepare for a clearly structured lesson.** Make sure that you have clearly defined learning objectives for each session, which identify the goals towards which you are striving. These should be monitored and reviewed regularly, for example in the UK against National Curriculum programmes of study.

2   **Clarify for pupils your expectations for each session.** Tell them what you expect them to be learning or practising within that period of study, and ensure this links with your overall plan. This need not provide a rigid template for activity, but should provide a framework with which you can vary activities to fit the occasion.

3   **Remember to set differential goals for pupils, according to their ability or prior experience.** Pupils all need to be extended and challenged: if you set identical work for all, this will satisfy few.

4   **Ensure that the pace and timing of the lessons are appropriate.** It helps if you vary activities within a session, so that interest and motivation are maintained, and so that pupils experience a variety of activities. A series of well-paced, brisk activities, with clearly defined deadlines for the class, helps pupils to achieve more fully.

5   **Aim to involve pupils in their own learning.** This can be achieved by asking pupils to consciously think about their own learning processes, and to become involved in setting personal targets. In this way, pupils

develop autonomy and lifelong learning skills which enable them to move on to further study or employment more confidently.

6 **Provide for pupils a visible means of demonstrating their own progress.** This could take the form of a chart or planner which pupils can mark in when particular milestones have been achieved. These are also effective means of helping pupils to develop their time management skills.

7 **Set targets against previous achievements.** If possible, ensure that each pupil is able to maximise potential by reviewing previous performance, setting interim goals, monitoring outcomes, and offering feedback. Use this information to set future targets.

8 **Remember that pupils of different gender may need different styles of management.** In the UK, there are noticeable trends whereby boys tend to underperform, producing less-well-presented work, having poorer self-organization skills, and taking work less seriously. To raise achievement, you may need to set for boys shorter, more-specific goals, with closer monitoring, and stronger structuring of tasks.

9 **Integrate the setting of homework into curriculum planning.** Ensure that homework relates to classroom tasks, has specific measurable outcomes, and generally challenges pupils. Encourage pupils to make use of a personal planner, as part of a means to ensure that they take responsibility for their own workloads and achievements.

10 **Make sure that literacy skills are reinforced across the curriculum.** All teachers should take responsibility for assuring high standards of presentation, spelling, punctuation and grammar. In addition, an awareness of subject-specific vocabulary needs to be inculcated in all classes.

11 **Integrate assessment into learning.** Make sure that assessment tasks link fully with stated learning goals, and ensure that performance criteria are specific, achievable, transparent and available. Assessment tasks will help students to achieve fully when they are pitched at the right level, neither too undemanding, nor too difficult to mitigate against a reasonable chance of success.

12 **Aim to promote an ethos of achievement in the classroom.** Aim to ensure that high standards are not just an aspiration, but are an expectation. Pupils with high ambitions to reach their own full potential are most likely to be successful when teachers continuously set high standards as a norm.

Chapter 2   Planning and assessment

Assessment is a really crucial area of any teacher's work and one that can have a key influence on the ways in which pupils develop and improve. We too are subject to assessment ourselves from time to time, formally through inspection and less formally but equally importantly when we get feedback on our work from our pupils.

Assessment is one of the most powerful driving forces for learning. It is often the case that pupils (and students in general) don't get down to serious learning unless some form of assessment is coming up. A danger is that in our efforts to help pupils to learn everything that is important, we assess too much, giving both our pupils, and ourselves, an intolerable burden of work. Much has been written on assessment in schools that we do not intend to replicate here: instead we offer a few suggestions on how to cope with what many teachers see as the most arduous chore of our professional lives!

Among the issues we mention in this chapter is that of implementing new structures in our educational provision. While such innovations are taking place (sometimes painfully) in many parts of the world, the particular structure we have selected to form the basis of some specific suggestions is the implementation of GNVQ (General National Vocational Qualifications) in England and Wales.

11

Assessing pupils' work

It often feels that we spend more time marking pupils' work than teaching them. This is probably no bad thing, providing pupils are gaining much from the feedback we give them. The following suggestions may help you enhance this feedback, and at the same time ease your marking load.

1   **Work out exactly what you are intending to measure.** Sometimes there will be a less time-consuming way to go about assessing pupils' work. For example, you don't need a full essay to measure their ideas about a topic; an essay plan or list of bullet points may show their ideas just as well, yet be far quicker for them to do, and for you to mark.

2   **Prepare, and share, marking schemes.** When designing assessed tasks for pupils, work out in advance the marking scheme you will use to assess their work, and give them clear pointers about what will gain them marks. There is clear evidence that the more pupils know about how assessment works, the better the standard of work they produce.

3   **Let pupils contribute to the assessment criteria.** From time to time, involve pupils themselves in the task of working out marking schemes for their work, and use their suggestions in your assessment of their work.

4   **Design tasks which are straightforward to assess.** Save yourself time and energy by making it easier to mark pupils' work. For example, it is much quicker to mark their answers to printed short-answer or completion questions, or multiple choice tests, than to work through a pile of essays.

5   **Explore the possibilities of computer-marked tests or exercises.** The use of computer-delivered assessment has grown rapidly in the last few years, and you can save yourself a lot of boring, routine marking by using it. The computer can also be used to give feedback responses to your pupils, either during or at the end of the test, and can work out for you the class scores lists.

6   **Keep clear records.** Design your own grids so you can see at a glance the performance of all of the pupils in a class. These can alert you to those pupils falling behind in their work, and can be very useful at parent–teacher interviews.

7   **Make room for your own feedback.** For example, get pupils to pencil in a fairly substantial margin at one side of the paper, or even to pencil off a feedback comments box at the foot of each page.

8   **Be aware of pupils' feelings when receiving assessed work back.** Remember that the moment that pupils get back some marked work is a time of heightened emotion for them. This means that they can be particularly sensitive to any comments you have written on their work, especially the first comments they read.

9   **Remember the importance of scores or grades.** When you give pupils a score or a grade, this is the first thing they look for and will dominate their reactions to your comments on their work. If the score is high, they may ignore most of your feedback comments. If the score is low they may be so dispirited that they don't read any feedback comments at all. Decide whether giving a score is important, or whether it may be worth giving feedback comments only at first, and working out the scores later.

10 **Be careful with the crosses.** Remember how demotivating crosses beside mistakes or wrong answers can be. Similarly, crossed-out words (for example where spelled wrongly) can be discouraging. Explore other ways of showing pupils their mistakes, such as using a fluorescent highlighter pen to pick out words and phrases, with margin notes giving explanations.

11 **Look for better things than ticks.** Ticks are good news for pupils, but it's often worth adding some positive feedback comments such as 'good point', 'nicely put', 'well done', which are even more encouraging.

12 **Give pupils the chance to redeem a poor assessment.** For example, use schemes where the best five-out-of-eight assessments make up the coursework grade.

12

Giving pupils face-to-face feedback

Face-to-face feedback to pupils can be very powerful and productive, but it can also be traumatic both for them and for us. The following suggestions may help you to maximize the benefits of such feedback, while minimizing the dangers.

1   **Remember pupils' feelings.** Remember that pupils can feel quite tense when getting face-to-face feedback from a teacher. They may see us both as experts and authority figures. The tension can cause them to receive our feedback in a distorted way, where they take our words beyond the actual messages we wish to convey.

2   **Use the benefits of face-to-face feedback.** Face-to-face feedback can give pupils much more information than written feedback, through facial expression, tone of voice, body language.

3   **Beware of the lost impact.** The main problem with face-to-face feedback is that it is transient. This means that pupils can't reflect objectively on this sort of feedback, as human nature means that they will remember particular parts of the feedback and forget other parts.

4   **Don't forget the dangers of subjective reactions.** Pupils' states of mind can affect their receptiveness to face-to-face feedback. If they happen to be feeling positive and optimistic at the time, they may remember the positive parts of your feedback, while if they are feeling tense or negative at the time, the parts they will remember most will be the critical things you tell them.

5   **Check that your messages are getting across.** An advantage of face-to-face feedback is that you can observe at once the effect that your words are having on pupils. When you can tell that your message is not yet getting across, you can go into more detail.

6   **Decide what to tell individuals, and what to share with groups.** It's worth deciding when best to give face-to-face feedback to individual pupils, and when to give feedback to pupils in groups. Highly specific feedback is best saved for one-to-one interviews, but it can be worth giving general feedback about common mistakes to groups rather than individuals.

7   **Prepare a written summary.** When you have a lot of feedback to give pupils (particularly to a whole class rather than individuals), it is useful to prepare summary notes of the main points you wish to convey. You may even be able to duplicate these notes, and give them out as permanent reminders of your main points.

8   **Always start and end on a high note.** Sometimes, face-to-face feedback will necessarily be hard to take by your pupils. On such occasions, try to make sure that you have some positive things to say about their work, and start and end with such points.

9   **Watch for the effects on pupils.** A strong advantage of face-to-face feedback is you can judge the effect it is having on pupils, from their facial expressions and body language. If they appear to be particularly sensitive to your comments, you can soften your approach accordingly.

10 **Face-to-face feedback is always two-way.** Exploit the opportunity of using face-to-face feedback occasions to find out more from your pupils about how they feel their learning is going. Asking questions such as 'why do you think you're finding this difficult?' can be useful.

13

Getting feedback from pupils

Your teaching will be more effective if you are aware of what the pupils' responses and future needs are. It is easy to go through the day without being self-reflective about your work – most of the time you are too busy! But try to make some time to reflect on how your pupils are responding to the work and whether you are having any success.

1   **Look everywhere for feedback.** The expressions on pupils' faces are an immediate source of feedback. The way they respond to your tasks and instructions is feedback. You can quickly tell whether they are enthusiastic about something, or bored by it.

2   **Ask pupils for general feedback.** Ask open-ended questions. Allow pupils time to work out exactly what the questions mean, and to respond without feeling embarrassed or intimidated. For example, ask them which part of a topic they like most, and why, and which part they find hardest, and why.

3   **Help pupils give you specific feedback.** Discuss their work with them on a one-to-one basis with the work in front of you. When they have a problem with part of their work, give them the chance to explain why they think the problem is there.

4   **Collect evidence of pupils' views and opinions.** Occasionally give out evaluation sheets or questionnaires designed to seek their feedback on specific issues.

5   **Don't make a big thing of 'silly' feedback.** There will always be someone who can't resist giving non-serious answers to evaluation questions. Concentrate on the feedback that is useful.

6   **Accept positive feedback.** Resist the urge to shrug off compliments. Give pupils who have positive things to tell you the satisfaction of knowing that their feedback is being received, not stifled.

7   **Accept negative feedback too!** Cultivate the attitude that there is no such thing as criticism, just feedback. Be willing to listen, and to help to draw out any negative feedback from pupils. Better still, thank them for their comments, for example saying 'I'm glad I now know about this, I'll give it further thought, thanks'.

8   **Help pupils to feel that their comments and ideas are valuable.** Ask for positive and constructive criticism on a particular aspect of the course – explain that you might be redesigning it for future classes.

9   **Collect feedback from groups as well as individuals.** You are less likely to get unconsidered feedback from a group than from an individual. Ask pupils to discuss their work in small groups and ask each group to report back to the rest of the class about how they think their work is progressing.

10   **Get further feedback from your colleagues.** When asked, colleagues are often able to give us further feedback about what they've gathered from pupils about our teaching.

14

Using self- and peer-assessment

The main advantages of using self-assessment and peer-assessment are that pupils find out more about how the assessment system works, and become better able to adjust their approaches to gain credit for their learning. The following suggestions may help you take advantage of these benefits.

1　**Help pupils to see the benefits of measuring their own work,** as a means of looking more deeply at what they have done.

2　**Equip pupils with a set of assessment criteria that they understand** and can apply to their work. Where possible, involve pupils themselves in working out the best way of wording the criteria, to give them a sense of ownership of the assessment agenda.

3　**Never mind the score, feel the learning!** Advise pupils self-assessing their own work that the most important outcome is not the score or mark they award themselves, but the decisions they make as they apply assessment criteria to their work.

4　**Trust pupils' judgement.** Avoid the reaction that pupils engaged in self-assessment will be far too kind to themselves. While *some* pupils may do this, most are rather harder on their own work than we ourselves may have been.

5　**Don't interfere lightly.** Rather than re-mark pupils' self-assessed work and give them 'our' scores as a comparison, it is better to give them feedback on the quality of their own self-assessment, and ask them to adjust their assessments on the basis of this feedback.

6 **Use peer-assessment for increased feedback.** Engaging pupils in peer-assessment (where they mark each other's work) can be even more beneficial than self-assessment at times, because of the thinking that pupils do as they apply assessment criteria to their classmates' work, and then check that the criteria have been applied correctly to their own work.

7 **Select appropriate tasks for peer-assessment.** Choose with care the nature of the tasks where pupils peer-assess each other's work. The most suitable tasks are those where pupils can benefit a lot from the informal feedback they can give each other about the work.

8 **Be available as an expert witness.** When pupils are in the process of peer-assessing, offer to give 'judgements' on particular issues, making sure that all pupils are aware of these finer points regarding the interpretation of the assessment criteria.

9 **Allow for re-negotiating of peer-assessed scores.** Act as adjudicator when pupils feel that their scores have been rated too low (though don't expect them to complain if they have been rated too high!).

10 **Don't be thought to be abdicating your responsibilities.** Be careful not to impose self-assessment or peer-assessment against pupils' will. They need to be convinced of the benefits for them in terms of deeper learning, otherwise they may feel that you are ducking out of something that they feel is your job.

15

Making sense of new structures

Introducing new course structures can seem a nightmare. For example, in the UK, moving into GNVQ programmes is an uphill struggle if you have not previously taught in vocational education, so we will take GNVQ as our example in the suggestions we make in this section. A different philosophy prevails – and as in most teaching, if you can understand the methods of assessment you will soon be able to cope with ways to present the content. In particular, the key to GNVQs lies in pupils accumulating appropriate *evidence* of their achievements as matched against the performance criteria outlined in the specifications.

1   **Ensure that the performance criteria to be met are clearly identified to the pupils.** Make these clear to pupils, when you set them tasks and assignments. Where necessary, translate the 'official' performance criteria into words which pupils can understand easily.

2   **Ensure that the tasks set will generate the evidence needed if carried out properly.** Give a range of examples to pupils, to help them see the sorts of evidence they should aim to accumulate as they work through GNVQ programmes.

3   **Plan to cover Optional Units at the same time as Mandatory Units where this is possible.** In particular, help to reinforce the connections between things pupils do for Optional Units and Mandatory Units.

4   **Help pupils see how a particular task can relate to several parts of their GNVQ programme.** Spend time mapping out where more than one performance criteria, aspect of the range, or Unit can be covered simultaneously.

5   **Encourage pupils to cross-reference their own work on a GNVQ programme.** Give them help in identifying performance criteria and achievements as they do them rather than retrospectively. Make sure that pupils have their own copies of the GNVQ documentation, and help them make sense of the terminology where necessary!

6   **Record examples of pupils' attainment in Key Skills as they happen.** Make a note explaining the skill displayed and the date. This can act as hard evidence of attainment. Encourage pupils to offer spontaneous alternative examples of work they have done which demonstrates their 'Key Skills' achievements.

7   **Set short deadlines for the completion of Units.** It is always easier to progress if you can establish early on what has already been covered, and have plenty of time left for things which are still outstanding.

8   **Encourage peer assessment and group discussion.** Try to do this when pupils attain the performance criteria across the range required. Get pupils to help each other in tracking their coverage of the range and performance criteria, and in keeping their logbooks up to date.

9   **Pay particular attention to the nature of 'good' evidence.** When pupils know 'what it looks like to have been shown to have succeeded', they can focus their efforts accordingly.

10   **Avoid feeling alienated by the GNVQ Specifications!** We can all think of other things that we feel should have been included in such specifications, and things that are included that we think are irrelevant. We can indeed adjust our teaching to cover the things we believe should be there, but at the end of the day, we need our pupils to be able to present evidence which matches the Specifications as they are.

16

Planning schemes of work

As you know, thorough planning is essential in the modern classroom if you are to succeed in covering all aspects of the National Curriculum. It will become second nature to you to spend a great deal of time on this aspect of your work. But make sure you leave some room for manoeuvre – teachers perform best when they are really interested in the topic, or when they digress to cover something which is particularly relevant on that day. Give yourself leeway to adapt your schemes of work to react to topical issues and enjoy fitting what the pupils need to know to what you care about!

1   **Don't make unrealistic plans.** Although an overall plan for the whole school year is necessary, it is not wise to plan in detail for more than a few weeks ahead. If you do this, the chances are that circumstances may change and your planning may be inappropriate. One of the features of a good scheme of work is adaptability.

2   **Ask yourself what skills are to be learned and what knowledge to be gained by the pupils.** Think about this before starting to formulate detailed plans. It is, after all, their learning outcomes that are the basis of any effective plan.

3   **Ensure that your teaching aims and objectives are clearly stated.** You may find it useful to re-compose these aims and objectives following the phrase: 'what this really means for my pupils is ...'.

4   **Think in advance of the ability range you expect.** Make sure that your plans allow highly able pupils to flourish, but also accommodate the needs and competences of less able pupils.

5   **Plan your assessments as early as possible.** Indicate the types of assessment you intend to use. Make sure that the things that are to be assessed link demonstrably to the aims and objectives you intend your pupils to achieve. Bring variety into your assessment processes, so that pupils with different abilities have their own chance to show themselves at their best in one or other form of assessment.

6   **Specify what the expected outcomes will be.** This is best done in terms of the evidence which pupils will be expected to provide to demonstrate their achievement of the objectives. Work out which of the outcomes will be assessable, and how you will approach assessing them.

7   **Include coverage of cross-curricular themes and dimensions where appropriate.** Incorporate issues such as equal opportunities, economics, business awareness and citizenship where appropriate, and highlight the coverage in your planning and schemes of work.

8   **Identify what resources will be needed and when.** This is best done at the planning stage, to allow time to obtain particular resources relating to individual objectives and learning outcomes.

9   **Plan the time scale for covering the objectives.** It is often best to cover as much as possible during the first half of a teaching year, to allow ample time for revision and consolidation of pupils' achievements well before final assessments are made.

10   **Acknowledge your own professional instincts and experience.** When teaching to 'a formula', it is all too easy to feel devalued and disenfranchised. However, with a bit of planning, it is often possible to mould your own knowledge of how you would like to teach a subject, and match it into even the most rigid-looking framework.

17

Invigilating internal exams

Sitting written exams is one of the most stressful parts of life for many pupils. Because of the need to prevent cheating and ensure a quiet environment, exam rooms are all the more hostile! Invigilating exams can be very tedious, but it is a highly responsible part of your work. If candidates get away with cheating, it will be regarded as your fault. The following suggestions may help you to invigilate fairly and kindly. (Remember that there will be specific regulations for external exams.)

1 **Minimize the possibilities of pupils cheating.** Tell them to leave bags in a pile at the front of the room, and before starting the exam remind them to double-check that they have nothing on their person that could be interpreted as a crib. Remind them to check pockets and pencil cases.

2 **Get your timing right,** Ensure that examinations start and finish promptly, and keep pupils informed verbally about the progress of time. Occasional comments such as 'one hour left to go', '30 minutes left', and so on can help pupils who have lost track of the progress of time.

3 **Try not to intimidate nervous pupils.** Be as unobtrusive as you can, while maintaining your vigilance. You will often see more by positioning yourself behind the candidates, in an aisle.

4 **Keep pupils well supplied with paper.** Walk round occasionally carrying extra paper, and when you can see that a pupil is about to need more, provide some without the pupil needing to ask.

5 **Keep records of the seating arrangement.** If when marking scripts it becomes suspected that some pupils have succeeded in collaborating, the seating records can often disprove or point further towards the suspicion.

6 **Act quickly but quietly if you find pupils cheating.** Write on the front of their scripts an appropriate note (for example: 'Incident at 09.42, involving also Janet Davies'), and make your own notes about exactly what you saw, and what you may suspect.

7   **Have arrangements in place for pupils who need the toilet.** If you're invigilating alone you can't leave the classroom or exam hall personally to escort such pupils there, but you can have a system where there is someone you can call in to see to such events.

8   **With externally-set papers, follow the Exam Board regulations to the letter.** In particular, ensure that candidates' scripts bear their names or candidate numbers as required, and that any loose sheets or graphs are fully identifiable.

9   **Be kind and supportive to pupils suffering from exam stress.** Even a smile from you can help relieve their stress. Sometimes you may need to enable a very tense pupil to be taken from the room for an escorted breath of fresh air. Highly tense or faint-feeling pupils may feel less stressed if they take their exam right at the back of the room, where they feel fewer eyes are on them.

10   **Be ready to solve problems arising from the question-paper.** With internal papers, if pupils bring to your attention a mistake or omission in a question, alert the whole group to leave this question alone for the time being, and send for the teacher who wrote the question to adjudicate. With external papers, it may be possible to arrange for someone to telephone the Exam Board.

18

Writing reports

This is always a tedious business, coming as it does often at the end of a busy term. You may have hundreds of reports to write on pupils you may only see once a week and you may be short of time to do it in. However, to each parent theirs is the only one that matters. To do each pupil justice, you need to prepare continuously for report-writing, rather than leave it till the last minute. It's a good idea if you are new to the job to check out the school policy on reports.

1   **Keep careful notes about each pupil's achievements throughout the year.** This will save you time later. File and record all of their marked work so you can base your report on clear evidence rather than estimation.

2   **When you are inexperienced, write your reports out in rough first.** Then transfer them onto the requisite sheets when you are satisfied with them. This will slow you down initially, but will help you to avoid errors and problems, especially when you are writing composite reports with other teachers.

3   **Make sure when you refer to a pupil by name, that you get it right!** If a pupil is generally known by a shortened version of the name, using this can make the report less formal.

4   **Make reports constructive.** Try to use each report as an opportunity to give advice on how the pupil can improve, rather than just a means of passing judgement.

5   **Be sensitive regarding whom the report is going to.** Don't assume that everyone lives in a nuclear family. If parents live apart, it is helpful to let both have copies of the report.

6   **Make sure that what you write is readable and accurate.** If the report is handwritten, make sure that your writing is up to it. If you use a typewriter or word processor, make sure that the print quality is acceptable, not too

faint, and contains no typographical errors. Check and double-check your spelling: nothing gives parents a worse impression than a teacher who cannot spell! (One of us always remembers an entry on his own report: 'spelling dissappointing!')

7   **Don't use a statement bank clumsily.** Many teachers have a range of comments and sentence elements that they use over and over again for different reports. This can be usefully formalized into a statement bank on a computer or in the mind, so that elements can be called up and combined in different ways to suit each pupil and each report. If this is sensitively done, it can save you time, but beware of writing reports which look as if they have been assembled by a robot. You will need to customize them for each individual pupil if they are not to be meaningless.

8   **Don't try to do too many reports at a time.** Do them in batches so they don't all end up being made of the sorts of banal clichés or unexceptional comments which can come from our brains when they're tired! Do try not to leave writing reports till the last minute.

9   **Respect pupils' rights to privacy.** Don't leave reports lying around in places where they can be read by anyone.

10   **Try to avoid surprises.** It may be helpful to let pupils know what you have written about them before their reports go home, especially if the news is bad. Security of transmission of the report to parents or guardians will need to be assured.

19

Preparing for an inspection

The thought of an imminent inspection can be intimidating and stressful to the classroom teacher and often the feeling within the school as the date nears can approach panic. However, an inspection can be a valuable experience in helping you to set priorities and identify your own areas of concern. If you are well prepared and have a clear idea of your objectives as a teacher there should be no worries! These suggestions, however, cannot possibly cover everything that the OFSTED handbook can cover – we simply give a few hints on how to approach the ordeal!

1   As a member of a department, **ensure that all the necessary policies and documentation are in place** as part of the pre-inspection evidence. If you are aware of areas of concern make sure that you have identified them as a department and have some strategy in place to begin to tackle them.

2   Ensure that any **departmental policies are in line with whole school policies,** for example, on assessment, equal opportunities, or discipline.

3   **Ensure that all the written policies are actually being implemented** and that all colleagues are aware of their practical application. Try to gather evidence of the implementation of each policy, so you can add detail to the rhetoric when necessary.

4   **Make sure that you have a clear idea of what you are doing and why** – both on a long-term and short-term basis! Make links between the way you go about your day-to-day work with pupils, and the whole-school policies and aims.

5   **Have clear, written schemes of work and individual lesson plans** which show how what you are teaching fits into the National Curriculum programmes of study or external examination syllabuses.

6   **Make it clear how what you do can be measured.** Ensure that what you are teaching – and what pupils are learning – can be assessed, and make it clear how and when this will happen.

7   **Be ready to show how you approach mixed-ability groups.** Ensure that your lessons are differentiated to meet the needs of pupils of all abilities.

8   **Be prepared to demonstrate variety.** Get in the habit of teaching structured lessons which allow for a range of activities and learning experiences.

9   **Be ready to show that you are well-prepared and resourced.** Ensure that adequate resources are available and accessible by pupils – label your drawers, stores, bookshelves, and so on. Demonstrate that pupils have access to facilities for independent learning.

10   **Be prepared to demonstrate the breadth as well as the depth!** Try to identify where you can cover cross-curricular themes and dimensions within your subject teaching and build this into your planning.

Chapter 3　Using teaching and learning resources well

The resources we use for our teaching are a crucial element in influencing the quality of our teaching. Outstandingly good teaching materials are not a copper-bottom guarantee of good teaching, but they do tend to improve the teacher's confidence and they tend to be an area of work that pupils comment on, whether adversely or with praise. Most teachers also recognize that the ways in which resources are used makes all the difference, and that planning of activities is crucial to their success. However well designed some learning resource materials may be, the learning pay-off which pupils derive is only as good as the briefings that we give pupils about how best to get what they need from the materials. Here we provide some guidance on the preparation and use of teaching and learning materials to support effective teaching. We cover computer-based and electronic resources separately, and in more detail, in Chapter 7.

20

Preparing interesting handout materials

With the availability of photocopiers and offset litho printing, it is increasingly preferable to use handout materials rather than relying on class-issued text books. The following suggestions may help you create handouts which are used actively by pupils, rather than simply filed away with their notes. Of course, you may need to collect in and re-use handouts where resources are limited. In such cases it may pay you to laminate the handouts.

1   **Try to make handouts look attractive and interesting.** Where possible, include pictures and illustrations, so that the materials are attractive for pupils to use. A box or edging makes all the difference.

2   **Make it clear what each handout is about.** Use clear headings so that pupils can quickly identify each handout. It can be worth having a numbered set of handouts, and a separate index page so that pupils can file them in the correct order when the set is complete.

3   **Present the objectives.** Start each handout with a clear statement of what the handout is for in terms of the things pupils will be able to do once they have worked through the handout. Such statements can convey the intended objectives of the handout, or the expected learning outcomes.

4   **Use handouts in an interactive way.** Include tasks and activities for pupils to do as they work through the handouts. These can include things to be done in class, and also things to be done as homework tasks.

5   **Provide white space for pupils to write on.** Include boxes for pupils to write in their answers to questions in the handouts. When pupils have their own writing on handouts, it adds to their sense of ownership of them.

6 **Organize your collection of handouts.** Keep a separate file containing the master copy of each handout, and separate files or boxes containing copies of each handout for issue to pupils.

7 **Share your resources.** Make an additional set of copies of your handouts available to other colleagues, in a central location such as a staff-room filing cabinet. Encourage colleagues to share their own handouts in a similar way.

8 **Make handouts which help pupils who are absent.** Create special handouts covering the most important topics in your subject, suitable for pupils who miss important lessons. These handouts may also be useful as revision aids for all pupils nearer their exams.

9 **Build assessment into handouts.** Include self-tests towards the end of each handout, so that pupils can check for themselves how much they already understand, and how much further work they may need to do on the materials.

10 **Make it easy to update handouts.** If possible, have your handout materials stored on computer-disc or desktop publishing systems, so that you can continuously make minor adjustments and improvements to the handouts, without having to re-compose them from scratch.

21

Preparing learning packages

Open or flexible learning packages have many advantages, including that they can allow pupils to work though selected parts of the curriculum at their own pace, in their own way, and where and when they want to work on them. The following suggestions may help you to design packages of your own, or make good use of existing ones with your pupils.

1   **Work out what pupils can do by themselves.** Identify the parts of the curriculum which may lend themselves best to pupils learning them using learning packages rather than taught lessons.

2   **Make the objectives clear.** Work out clear statements of the intended learning outcomes of learning packages you design or use. Make sure that pupils understand exactly what they are aiming to be able to do as a result of working through each learning package.

3   **Design packages around things for pupils to do – not just to read.** Ensure that learning packages contain plenty of activity for pupils. Make sure that the tasks and activities in the packages are clearly phrased, and that pupils understand exactly what they are supposed to do.

4   **Package up your feedback as well as the activity.** Make sure that each time pupils have a go at a task or activity, there is readily available feedback, so that they can self-assess their work. The feedback may be provided in print in the packages (out of sight of the task questions), or could be delivered personally by you.

5   **'Why did I get this wrong?'** Remember that pupils don't only need to know whether or not they approached a task correctly – if they got it wrong, they need guidance as to what went wrong. Check that the feedback they receive covers this.

6   **Learning packages aren't textbooks.** Make it clear to pupils how learning packages are not like textbooks. Learning packages are things for them to do, not just to read. They will learn much more from having a go at the tasks and activities, than just from reading the information in the packages.

7   **Test out the bits of your package.** Experiment with components of learning packages in class, where you can monitor how pupils handle them. Take particular note of problems pupils have, and add extra guidance to the packages on the basis of this.

8   **Measure what is happening.** Include or add an end-test of one kind or another, which pupils will hand in for marking when they finish working through a package. Use this not only to check their achievements, but to identify any trouble-spots in the learning package.

9   **Give pupils guidance.** When using an existing learning package, it can be well worth adding a brief set of guidance notes 'how to approach using this package', highlighting the most important parts of the package, and the best ways of tackling it.

10   **Show pupils where the package fits into their overall course.** Remember to make sure pupils know how much the things they learn using learning packages count for in their overall course.

22

Getting the most from the library

School libraries and learning resources rooms may contain large amounts of useful information; the problem is helping pupils to make the most of them. Don't assume that pupils know how to use libraries or have often visited them. The following suggestions may help them make good use of such resources. Please see Chapter 7 for suggestions about how to help pupils to use non-print resources, some of which are often to be found in modern libraries.

1 **Spell out the benefits to pupils.** Explain to pupils how useful it is to become good at tracking down relevant information in libraries (public libraries as well as at school). Explain how much time it can save them, when finding information to use in writing essays or reports.

2 **Give pupils useful practice.** Set tasks or projects which require pupils to track down particular reference materials you know are in the library or resource centre. Plan the tasks so that pupils become familiar with the ways the materials are catalogued or indexed.

3 **Help pupils develop their searching skills.** Help pupils to develop their skills at focusing on the most relevant materials. Give them clear guidelines to help them know exactly what they are looking for in the materials they consult.

4 **Help pupils to get their references right.** Train pupils in the correct way to refer to the sources of information they quote. Make sure that in your own lessons and handouts you refer to materials precisely (for example: Saunders, D (ed.) (1994) *The Complete Student Handbook*, Blackwell, Oxford).

5 **Encourage groups of pupils to use the library.** Give pupils group exercises to do, using materials in the library, helping them to pick up from each other valuable tracking and retrieval skills.

6   **Value the expertise of library staff where you have them.** Remind pupils
     how useful the help they can receive from librarians can be. Many public
     or college libraries have subject librarians, who have a good understanding
     of their own subjects as well as excellent knowledge of the available books
     in the field.

7   **Encourage pupils to use their eyes in a library!** For example, when there
     are several copies of a book, or when particular books are well-thumbed,
     it is probable that these are more useful sources of information than an
     'unused-looking' book.

8   **Remind pupils that modern libraries don't just contain books.** They
     also contain audio-visual materials, CD-ROM databases, and computer-
     assisted learning packages. Many more details on how to optimize pupils'
     use of electronic and computer-based resources are given in Chapter 7.

9   **Encourage pupils to make useful notes** when using materials in a library
     or resource centre. Remind them to make careful notes of which sources
     they extract information from, so they can locate particular sources again
     quickly when they may need to.

10   **Alert pupils to the usefulness of contents pages and indexes** when
     working out whether a particular book is relevant to what they want to
     find out from it. This can be far quicker than simply scanning through the
     book itself.

23

Organizing resources

If your room is well organized and ordered, pupils are more likely to respond by tidying up themselves. Giving pupils access to resources also helps them to begin to take responsibility for their own learning and progress. Both you and your pupils will have a clearer idea of what is available by keeping stock labelled and sorted.

1   **Arrange well-used resources in easily accessible and labelled storage** so that pupils can help themselves, saving your time for more important tasks.

2   **Keep small items such as pencils, rulers, and so on in multiples of ten** so that you can easily check on numbers returned. Give responsibility for looking after certain items to a monitor who will give out and collect in books and other items – this saves traffic jams and needless wandering about.

3   **Ensure that there are plentiful supplies of scrap paper,** available for rough work and drafting. Cultivate local supplies of one-sided scrap paper, such as reprographics departments at local colleges or firms.

4   **Keep valuable or destructible resources locked away.** However, don't make it appear that these resources are unavailable to pupils; instead help them to see for themselves that they need to handle these resources with care.

5   **Use boxes, jars and trays to keep small items together.** A clear system of labels can turn a collection of boxes, jars and trays into an accessible resource collection.

6   **Emphasize the need to respect tools, materials and equipment** and the need to use them carefully and safely. It is easy for pupils to abuse resources simply because they do not feel any ownership or realize the value of such resources, or the difficulty in replacing certain items.

7   **Assemble collections of stimulus or source material in labelled boxes** so that pupils can track them down easily and use them independently.

8   **Collect together worksheets and other task-briefings** and keep in accessible storage for pupils who happen to finish work early, or to give them out as 'extension tasks' for more able pupils who may benefit from additional challenges.

9   **Try to make regular times when you sort out your materials and resources.** Weekly is ideal, but half-termly will do. The longer you leave it, the longer it will take you to sort them out ultimately.

10   **Require pupils to take responsibility for the resources they use.** Don't let them get away with sloppy return of materials or incorrect placing of resources. Getting them to take this responsibility necessarily means that you have to ensure that they are allowed sufficient time at the end of class to put things away properly before they rush off to their next session.

24

Making do with limited resources

Unfortunately this is an ever-more-important aspect of the job in these times of Formula Funding and restricted budgets. Teachers have become adept at managing with very little in many areas of the curriculum. So it pays to be aware right from the start that resources are not infinite. When it's gone it's gone!

1   **Keep a strict eye on stock;** always count in and out small items which are easily taken away (often without thinking). Get one of the more conscientious pupils to take responsibility for certain resources.

2   **Save expensive consumable items for special lessons or the culmination of a project.** Explain to pupils that such items are difficult or impossible to replace, and solicit their help in conserving and protecting them.

3   **Use scrap or recycled materials** – encourage the imaginative and creative use of such resources. Link this to lessons to be learned about environmental issues and conservation.

4   **Prepare your own worksheets and handouts.** This can be much less expensive than giving out published materials.

5   **Help pupils to value resources.** Make sure that pupils are taught the correct way to use materials and equipment and that they understand their cost.

6   **Invite pupils to contribute resources.** Rather than asking for donations, you can ask the class to bring along for the day particular things that may help in the particular lessons to be conducted. Make a 'shopping-list' of resources which would be useful, and ask pupils to put their names besides any items they could bring along. (Make sure, however, that disadvantaged pupils are able to contribute something useful, and don't feel excluded).

7   **Beg, borrow and steal!** Much as it goes against the grain for professional people who believe that their profession should be adequately resourced, when times are hard, any solution is better than none! When you know exactly what you need, it's well worth asking local businesses or organizations if they can help provide some things on your 'wanted' list.

8   **Use outside sources.** For example, the British Association for the Advancement of Science provides a service of free talks to pupils by practising scientists, who will often bring along a range of expensive equipment to use in demonstrations.

9   **Maintain good contacts with local colleges.** It is often possible to arrange for a school party to visit a college at no charge, for a day which includes opportunities for pupils to use equipment that would not be available at school.

10 **Find out what is available from large companies.** Several large organizations provide a range of education booklets and videos, as part of their promotion policies. These materials are usually available on request, at no charge, and can provide the basis of useful class activities.

25

Making your classroom into an attractive learning environment

Secondary schools can often seem alien, impersonal environments where only serious business goes on. Take some tips from primary teachers and put some effort into making your room your own space – after all you will be spending a good chunk of your life there!

1   **Choose strong, bright and warm colours** if you are given any chance to have your say about the decor. Pupils appreciate such colours much more than the neutrals, and they really do notice! If the room is in need of decoration and funds are not available, use posters, coloured paper and remnants of fabrics to cover the messy bits. The use of different textures and materials can make a cold room much more welcoming.

2   **Display pupils' work to improve the surroundings.** Displays can be attractive and interesting, and visually stimulating, and are good educational practice anyway.

3   **Encourage pupils to bring in interesting pictures** to add to displays. They will feel a sense of ownership, and in this way will feel it is also their responsibility to look after their environment.

4   **Use plants to make the room look more attractive and personal.** If you have tutor groups in your room, involve them in taking responsibility for the care and watering of the plants.

5   **'Books do furnish a room'** – as well as being useful to read. They can make a classroom look more interesting. Use colourful designs on book jackets as part of your display – make the layout of the bookshelves accessible and welcoming by providing headings and illustrations.

6   **Carpets are (nearly) magic!** It is increasingly common now for classrooms to be carpeted, as it is often cheaper than vinyl; choose the option of carpets whenever you have the choice. It not only makes a classroom feel warmer and more pleasant, but it cuts down considerably on noise.

7   **Assemble interesting objects** as well as pictures in your room. You might choose these to relate to what you are teaching, or just because you like them. Unusual items can stimulate creative work in many areas.

8   **Do your own minor maintenance.** For example, if the door is squeaky, oil it. If the door shuts noisily, you may consider sticking the odd strip of draught-proofing strip strategically, to muffle the sound of the door closing.

9   **Rearrange the furniture.** With pupils help, you can make major transformations in the layout of a classroom quite quickly. They too will usually enjoy the change. It can also be a useful move when you feel that the class geography needs to be adjusted to disperse cliques.

10   **Keep an eye on your access.** Ideally, you need to be able to go right up to any pupils as they are working, to give them individual advice or feedback. Pupils who feel they are safely isolated from you may not do much work!

26

Making effective displays

Classrooms can be made visually interesting with displays of pupils' work and other materials which can stimulate and inform. Don't worry if you feel you have little artistic skill – if you follow a few guidelines you can make anything look attractive.

1   **Pupils' own work will usually be the focal point of a display.** Choose examples from across the ability range – one of the reasons for displaying work is to show that it is valued. If they have produced good work which is not well presented you can often get them to re-present it more clearly for a special display. Make sure you include pupils' names on their work.

2   **Include photographs, newspaper cuttings, artefacts, fabric, found objects** – anything to add colour, texture and interest. Pictures and other relevant information can make the display informative as well as visually stimulating. Examples of the work of others – writers, poets, scientists, illustrators and artists will also act as stimulus.

3   **Use the display to inform others of the work of your class** – add a few sentences of explanation about your aims and methods in producing the work.

4   **Involve your class in displaying their own work** – they will enjoy this and feel more ownership of the room. But don't forget to teach them what to do! However, often they will come up with original and exciting ways of doing it which should be encouraged and facilitated. Get them to word-process some of their work for display, and involve them in producing headings and illustrations.

5   **Strong, clear lettering is essential** – if you find lettering difficult (who doesn't!) try using a stencil or use computer-generated type. If you use a computer, beware of using too many different fonts in one display – two are generally plenty, and vary the effect by changing the size and style. Sometimes handwritten capitals (not bubble writing!) or italics can liven up a dull display. Use simple headings in bold lettering – underlining can look tacky.

6   **The choice of background is important** – if in doubt choose a strong dark colour (you can't go wrong with black sugar paper). If you want a coloured background pick out a predominant colour in the work to use. Mount light pieces of work on a dark ground and vice versa. If your paper is white and the background is light or medium in tone, it may help to draw a thick black line around the edge of the paper with a marker – this makes the work stand out and is cheaper and less time-consuming than double mounting.

7   If you are double mounting the work, **use a fairly thin border in a contrasting tone.** The size of the borders should be equal on the top and sides but slightly wider at the bottom – this avoids the illusion of the picture appearing to slide off the mount.

8   **It is best to have plenty of visual information on the display** – avoid vast areas of background scattered with small pieces of work. Line up the edges of the work to give an ordered look, or display work diagonally and sometimes overlap to give a more lively effect. Use different shapes – circles, ovals – to mount work on and vary the size of the work displayed.

9   **Change displays regularly.** They can rapidly become part of the scenery. Keep up running repairs to edges and eradicate graffiti – nothing looks worse than a scruffy display.

10 **Consider the use of borders to enhance the display** – choose an appropriate motif and repeat by stencilling or photocopying.

27

Taking pupils on a trip

School trips can be great fun and highly memorable, but they are a terrific responsibility and need meticulous planning. Make sure you are aware of the school or LEA guidelines for taking pupils out of school, and always follow these guidelines to the letter!

1   **Make sure that the parental permission forms go out well in advance.** File all their responses carefully.

2   **Give pupils (and parents) a detailed printed briefing for the trip.** Include full information about the itinerary, with times and places in case anyone should get separated from the group, and a telephone contact number for emergencies.

3   **Plan the visit thoroughly, with sufficient structured activities to keep the pupils occupied productively.** Boredom breeds disruptive behaviour. Use checklists, questionnaires and task sheets (not just written tasks) to help to focus pupils' activities.

4   **Make sure you don't lose pupils!** Count them in and out at all times, and delegate individual colleagues and any parent helpers to be responsible for small groups. Never let pupils wander off unsupervised.

5   **Ensure that pupils know the standards of behaviour expected of them before they set off.** This can save you having to set the rules for good behaviour in public situations. It is also worth setting out in advance any sanctions you may need to use when dealing with unsatisfactory behaviour by pupils.

6   **Have with you an emergency kit.** Include first aid equipment, disposable wipes, tissues, sick bucket or bags and so on, as well as spare pens, paper, and anything else you think appropriate.

7   **Let pupils know what they are expected to bring with them.** This includes the sort of clothing that will be suitable, any equipment they may need. Also set clear guidelines about what refreshments may be brought, and how much spending money is permitted.

8   **Be where you can see pupils.** When travelling on coaches, you will have better oversight of what pupils are up to if you travel towards the back of the coach, rather than up-front with the driver.

9   **Make productive use of travelling time.** Give pupils observation or discussion tasks, especially on the outward journey when excitement levels may be high.

10   **Follow up the trip.** Use activities back in the classroom that make best use of the on-site learning pupils may have done. Use assignments in the classroom which allow pupils to draw together what they have learned in the field. Display photos, maps, and pupils' work when appropriate to keep up the momentum well after the trip is over.

28

Visiting museums and art galleries

Visits to galleries and museums can be a most effective learning experience for pupils but they only work really well when adequately prepared. The visit should be the focal point of a topic of work, rather than an additional extra, because so much can result from the opportunity to see at first hand examples of what pupils are studying. The additional stimulus of new surroundings and being out of school can have tremendous benefits.

1   **Visit the museum or gallery beforehand.** Decide what you want the pupils to get out of the visit. Any such visit will usually cover many aspects of the curriculum and might be developed into a fully cross-curricular project. Set a few clear objectives for the visit which are integrated into the course of study being followed in school. If appropriate, prepare worksheets, quiz sheets or handouts using what you have learned from the preliminary visit.

2   **Book your party into the museum well in advance.** Talk to the Education Officer there about what facilities are on offer. Discuss the best time to visit, and how you will take advantage of any specialist help which may be available.

3   **Prepare your pupils well for what they will see and be doing.** Do this before the visit if possible, or even on the way to the venue. If possible show some slides or pictures of exhibits – stimulate their interest beforehand. Sometimes the way a museum or gallery presents itself can seem intimidating or boring to young visitors and they need to understand the reasons for and relevance of their visit.

4   **Plan the work you will do so that it can be developed further back at school.** Visits often take the form of research, stimulus or fact-finding, and more detailed finished work can be produced later.

5   **Allow enough time in the museum or gallery for some practical work.** This may include investigation, recording, and drawing. If left to their own devices pupils may go through the museum very quickly with an unfocused eye. On the other hand, sometimes an over-reliance on worksheet or quizzes can mean that they look only for the right answers and ignore any possibilities for individual exploration. Many museums have an Education Room where pupils can have a packed lunch or break, or do follow-up work, or listen to a talk.

6   **Split your class into small groups.** Where there is a lot to see, divide pupils into manageable groups to research certain aspects in detail and report back in school.

7   **Get the pupils to look critically at *how* the work or exhibits are displayed.** Also ask them to look critically at *what* is on display. Is there enough explanation offered to the public? Are the displays clearly ordered and attractively presented? You could get pupils subsequently to produce their own mini-gallery or museum in school for other pupils to visit.

8   **Try to arrange a short talk about the exhibits.** If possible, arrange for an expert or member of the museum staff to give such a talk. A new speaker, or acknowledged expert in a subject will often have more impact than their familiar class teacher.

9   **Arrange for the pupils to be allowed to handle or more closely examine some of the less valuable exhibits.** This can help to make pupils feel 'more special' than casual visitors to the gallery or museum. They could sketch or make notes of these exhibits in closer detail.

10 **Involve the pupils in displaying what they have done.** When the follow-up work is completed back at school, ask pupils to prepare their own display, bearing in mind the type of display techniques they saw in the museum and how the objects were presented.

Chapter 4 Supporting pupils' learning

Helping pupils to learn is what our job is all about. All too often the emphasis is on what is taught rather than what is learned, and this is exacerbated by an excessive emphasis on syllabuses and curriculum matters. Our experiences have led us to believe that study skills are less effective when they are provided as an additional 'bolt on' element of class work. Instead, we would argue that it is the job of teachers at all levels to think as much about how pupils are learning as about the content delivered. For this reason, the next section concentrates on how the teacher can help pupils to become more effective learners.

Further advantages of spending time on developing pupils' study-skills can be linked to the increasing recognition of the value of transferable skills (Key Skills) which are highly sought after by employers, and which will also help pupils to reach their full potential when they continue into further or higher education.

29

Helping pupils who don't read well

Not being able to read as well as those around one can seem to pupils like a major catastrophe – particularly in an education system that bases much of its assessment on pupils' skills in reading and writing. The following tips may help redress the balance a little.

1 **Say things as well as writing them.** When setting tasks, provide your briefing orally as well as in writing or print. Make it clear you don't mind repeating the task briefing again for anyone who wishes to *hear* it once more.

2 **Find out who needs help.** Try to identify pupils who have genuine problems with reading, and ensure that they get specialist help from those trained to diagnose and assist pupils with reading problems.

3 **Mind your language!** Use short sentences whenever possible in written tasks and instructions. Reading difficulties are often simply problems in the interpretation of long complex instructions. Consider how the subject-specific vocabulary you use may cause problems to those not familiar with it.

4 **Put reading into perspective.** Remind all pupils that skills in the use of words, and the interpretation of words, are only a small part of what it is to be a successful human being. Remind them that caring, compassion, humour and patience are in fact much more important qualities than the mere ability to use and interpret printed or written words.

5 **Make assessment less dependent on reading skills.** Vary the forms and processes of assessment you employ, so that success does not depend inordinately on pupils' ability to read and interpret written or printed questions. Use spoken questions and instructions as well.

6   **Use some tasks where reading is not too important.** Incorporate tasks and exercises which do not depend on reading skills. Where appropriate, single out pupils for praise, when you know of their problems with tasks which would have involved reading skills.

7   **Help pupils preserve their self-esteem.** Don't allow pupils with reading difficulties to think that they are 'mentally subnormal' or 'strange'. Keep in mind that it is probably just one small area of intelligence that they have problems with, and that they may be highly gifted in other areas.

8   **Help with spelling as well.** Pupils with reading problems often have difficulty with spelling. Identify new vocabulary and help pupils learn to spell new words. 'LCWC' (Look, Cover, Write and Check) is a useful technique for self-help. Spelling ability is not magic: it is essentially a visual skill.

9   **Help pupils to gain confidence and motivation.** Spend additional time with pupils who seem to have difficulties interpreting written or printed words. It can sometimes be the case that they just need reassurance and confidence-building.

10   **Never stop explaining.** Use 'WIRMI' – 'What it really means is ...' as a way of helping pupils put into their own words the meanings of longer sentences or instructions, and encourage pupils to compare interpretations with each other.

30

Helping pupils who don't do maths well

Many people (not least we teachers!) remember their time learning maths at school with little affection. Indeed, this can lead to feelings of mental block against anything numerical or algebraic. Probably, maths is the hardest subject of all to teach really well. The following suggestions focus on how maths is learned best. Try to make maths fun and accessible sometimes. With some imagination (and useful source books) everyday problems – Saturday wages, League Tables, timetables and darts scores can provide useful practice.

1   **Accept that numbers *are* a foreign language!** They can't be read in the same way as sentences, or heard in long sequences. When pupils have difficulties, try to find out if they understand the stages leading up to the points where their problems are. Maths is about building bricks and if a key brick is missing, the whole process is blocked.

2   **Celebrate mistakes!** Remind pupils that getting something wrong is as useful as getting it right, if the cause of the mistake can be tracked down and isolated. Give praise for each and every stage that is understood and done correctly.

3   **Help pupils detect mistakes for themselves.** From time to time, use a 'spot my mistakes' exercise on the blackboard (or in handout materials). Plan to show pupils the most likely sorts of mistakes they may make, giving them the opportunity to identify the mistakes without the embarrassment of having made them themselves. Develop pupils' feel for the right sort of answer (estimates) so that they become better at recognizing answers which are silly.

4   **Remind pupils of the importance of practice.** Maths is learned by doing maths – not watching someone else do it. Include plenty of practice to help pupils consolidate things they have just learned.

5   **Never mind the speed, is the answer right?** Be careful not to place too much value on speed. Pupils who can do something successfully but slowly, are in a position to speed up in due course, but may become entirely demotivated if they feel under immediate pressure to get things right quickly.

6   **Give pupils the chance to learn by explaining.** Let pupils who have got something right explain to others exactly how they did it. They can remember how they learned it themselves, and can often communicate this better than someone who has known it for a long time.

7   **Let pupils see how each other tried it.** It is useful to get pupils to mark each other's work in informal tests and exercises. This can alert them to the sorts of mistakes to avoid, as well as to the correct way to approach problems or tasks.

8   **Arrange competition between groups rather than between individuals.** Try getting pupils to work in threes, in a problem-solving game, where each trio is given a different problem (of a similar standard), and the trios compete as to which can solve the most problems in half an hour. There is often no 'right' means to getting the correct answer. Different pupils will understand and use different methods. Try to encourage this in your explanations and praise.

9   **Have practice material at hand.** Have a bank of handout sheets of problems to practise with available, and encourage pupils who need such practice to do them. Give different pupils different sheets, to avoid the wrong sort of collaboration.

10   **Work out your priorities.** For the majority of the class, it is probably more important to cover the basics soundly, rather than to digress into advanced maths. That said, have some difficult problems available to give to those pupils who will respond positively to the challenge.

31

Helping pupils to learn together

Pupils learn a great deal from each other. They often can understand something more easily when someone who has only just understood it is explaining it to them. Most pupils enjoy working in groups for at least some of the time. The following suggestions may help you get the most from group work.

1   **Be up front with pupils about your reasons for using group activities:** talk to them about the benefits of co-operative learning.

2   **Plan for collaboration rather than competition.** Devise group activities in which tasks can be shared out between group members and expertise can be shared.

3   **Help pupils help each other to learn.** Encourage pupils to quiz each other, giving them practice both in working out sensible questions to ask, and in answering questions informally.

4   **Involve pupils in each other's assessment.** At its simplest level, this could mean checking each other's answers against a model answer given by you. More sophisticated forms of peer assessment can be encouraged subsequently, with pupils giving each other feedback against given or negotiated criteria as their evaluative skills develop.

5   **Give pupils opportunities to teach one another:** teaching someone else something is an excellent way for them to consolidate their own learning (as we teachers know!).

6   **Use different kinds of groups.** When putting pupils into groups for collaborative activity, think about group formation. On different occasions you might like to put them into friendship groups, ability-based groups or learning teams, where you try to balance the range of skills and abilities in each group.

7   **Remain aware of feelings.** Be sensitive about coping with inter-personal problems within groups. There is no point forcing pupils to work together, if they cannot stand each other. It may be necessary to have contingency plans to change group formations if problems occur.

8   **Avoid passengers.** Monitor group activity to ensure that groups do not carry passengers, prepared to piggy back on the efforts of others.

9   **Distribute any burdens.** Change the composition of working groups at intervals so that any unpopular or difficult pupils are not always working in the same groups.

10   **Let groups share their products.** Let groups have opportunities to benefit from the learning of other groups through the use of display materials, presentations, and so on.

32

Helping pupils to revise effectively

Exams measure the quality of pupils' revision more than how long they spent revising. The following suggestions may help your pupils adopt effective and productive approaches to revision.

1 **Prepare revision aids.** All the way through a course, prepare summaries of main points (or get pupils themselves to do this), explaining that these will be useful for later revision, and that it is never too early to start learning from them.

2 **Help pupils know the agenda.** Prepare lists of short questions covering everything important about individual topics, and give these to pupils inviting them to become well-practised at answering the questions.

3 **Get pupils practising.** Use class games where pupils in groups quiz each other using lists of short questions, and keep scores. Suggest groundrules, such as that if the person who is asked a question cannot answer it, the person who asked it can gain the score for that question by answering it instead.

4 **Show the standards and structures.** Where pupils are heading towards exams, give out copies of old exam papers early in the course, so that they can see the structure of the exams, and the depth of typical questions.

5 **Let pupils in on how the typical examiner's mind may work.** From time to time, set a class exercise around an old exam question, then get pupils to mark each other's answers using the sort of assessment criteria which would have been used in the real exam.

6 **Help pupils adopt active strategies.** Remind pupils that simply reading something over and over again is a very slow and passive way of trying to learn it. Revision is only active when pupils are applying what they know, and using it to answer questions either in writing or orally.

7 **Help pupils see how they learn best.** Ask pupils how they learned things (anything at all) that they are already good at. Then remind them that the same processes (learning by practising, and learning from mistakes) can be deliberately applied to things they need to learn for exams.

8 **Encourage pupils to make and use summaries.** Help pupils to make their own concise summaries of the things they need to know. Help them decide what is important, and what is just background detail.

9 **Help pupils plan their revision tactics.** Suggest that it is better to do revision in frequent, short spells rather than long, continuous ones. Help pupils to make revision timetables when they are entered for public examinations or end-of-year exams. Remind pupils that everyone's concentration span is quite short, and it is how often they revise something that counts, rather than how long they spend on it in total.

10 **Variety is the spice of revision!** Encourage pupils not to spend too long trying to learn one topic, but to switch topics about every half-hour or so. A change is as good as a rest as far as our brains are concerned – and much more productive than letting boredom set in.

33

Helping pupils to pass exams

Success in exams is as much dependent upon sensible exam techniques as upon subject knowledge. It is sometimes difficult to give pupils sound advice when the system keeps changing, but the following suggestions are intended to help you assist your pupils in developing their exam techniques.

1   **Familiarity breeds confidence.** Especially when heading towards public exams, help pupils to become familiar with the layout and structure of real exam papers, by giving them class and homework opportunities to practise on questions from old papers.

2   **What is the nature of the game?** Remind pupils that exams essentially measure their skills at answering exam questions in writing, and that anyone can improve these skills simply by practising writing such answers.

3   **Stress the importance of good time management during exams.** Remind pupils that if they spend too long writing too much for question 1, and have no time left for the last two questions, they will have lost far more marks than if they'd done a short answer for question 1 and answered all the other questions.

4   **Help pupils to *analyse* old exam questions.** Ask them to work out what the questions really mean. Help them identify the key words in questions, including 'why?', 'what?', 'how?', 'when?', 'compare', 'explain', 'describe', 'discuss'.

5   **Stress the importance of wise decisions.** When pupils have a choice of questions to make, remind them how important it is to make wise choices concerning which questions they will attempt. The only way of doing this is to read each question slowly, carefully, and more than once.

6   **'Keep checking the questions'.** Suggest to pupils that they should re-read the question they're answering several times while writing their answers. This reminds them exactly what the question is asking, and helps them to avoid going off on tangents.

7   **'Show what you're trying to do'.** Emphasize that in numerical or problem-type questions it is important for examiners to be able to see exactly what pupils are trying to do in their answers. If examiners can see the point at which a mistake occurs, they can award marks for the other parts which are correct. If they can't see what went wrong, they can't give any marks at all.

8   **'Don't get stuck and have a mental blank!'** When pupils get stuck on a question because they have forgotten something, encourage them to move on to another question they can answer well, rather than becoming panic-stricken or tense. What matters most is scoring points across the whole paper, rather than getting a particular question entirely right.

9   **Remind pupils that examiners are human** – just like teachers – and like giving marks for correct answers. Examiners are not simply searching for mistakes. Examiners respond best to clear, well-set-out answers and well-reasoned arguments, and definite conclusions.

10   **'Save time for checking'.** Explain to pupils how useful it is to save several minutes towards the end of each exam, to re-read through everything they have written, correcting obvious mistakes, and adding important points that may have come to mind since writing the answers.

34

Helping pupils to be creative

It is all too easy when teaching to a syllabus or programmes of study to forget that the development of creative or imaginative qualities can also be enhanced by your own behaviour in the classroom. You may have a firm idea in your own mind of what you want to teach and may fall into the trap of leaving no leeway for new or unconventional thoughts. Sometimes when work is technically poor or badly presented we may miss its originality or unusual characteristics.

1   In setting a task or project **use a broad task briefing or a 'neutral stimulus'** so that pupils have plenty of scope for approaching the task in their own ways, and ensuring that differentiation is in the outcome of the activity.

2   **Accept innovation and individuality,** even if the solutions pupils deliver from your task briefings are not what you had in (your) mind.

3   If work is technically poor or if the presentation is weak, **react positively to the ideas and thoughts behind it** and help pupils to develop skills in self-expression.

4   **Ask open-ended questions and accept a range of answers.** Try to avoid asking questions to which you anticipate only one 'right' answer (unless you are dealing with matters of fact).

5   **Allow time for pupils to experiment, make mistakes and explore ideas.** When presenting pupils with a new area of work, new techniques or materials, give them a chance to explore possibilities and try things out before you launch into a major piece of work.

6   **Encourage the use of rough work books.** Pupils may often feel it is easier to be creative in rough books, and you can then help them redraft their original ideas in work where presentation is given their attention.

7   **Use brainstorming** with individuals, in small groups or as a whole class. Remind pupils that in brainstorming sessions, all ideas are valued and none criticized.

8   **Try to set open-ended tasks that encourage divergent rather than convergent outcomes.** This will not only be more interesting for your pupils, but also for you.

9   **Get pupils to work in groups on a range of ideas.** Don't ask them to pick the best of these, but ask them to find ways to incorporate the best elements of all of the contributions produced in the groups.

10 **Ask pupils to think about 'dream' and 'nightmare' solutions to problems.** What would this be like if everything went in the best possible way? Now what would it be like if everything went wrong? Help pupils to distil learning points from these activities and the scenarios they think of.

35

Helping pupils to write essays

In many formal examinations, pupils are required to put what they know into the form or written essays. In coursework too, pupils' skills at writing essays may count a lot. The following suggestions may help you to help them to approach this task successfully and effectively.

1   **Help pupils to plan essays.** Show them ways of mapping out the ideas they may subsequently turn into paragraphs in their final versions of an essay.

2   **Remind pupils to look carefully at the title or briefing.** We all know how easy it is to stray away from the main topic, and to end up writing things which (however interesting) are irrelevant to the task in progress.

3   **Help pupils to analyse what is required.** Remind them of the significance of such key words as 'how', 'why', 'when', 'where', and so on in essay briefings. In particular, alert pupils to what they should try to do when asked to 'compare' or 'contrast' or both.

4   **Remind pupils that it takes several drafts to write a good essay.** Encourage them to get their ideas down on paper, and then spend some time rearranging them before they come up with their 'final essay'.

5   **Help pupils to see the importance of firm conclusions.** Any essay usually requires the writer to come to some sort of conclusion – or at least to sum up what has been said. It is important that essays don't just stop in full flow, but arrive at a decisive ending.

6   **Help pupils make good introductions.** There is no better time to compose the introduction than when we know exactly what we're introducing! Suggest to pupils that they should write the introductions to their essays quite late, when they know exactly what their essays will have covered.

7   **Remind pupils of the usefulness of practice.** The best way to become better at writing essays is to write lots of them. Or better stills, to plan lots of them – it is possible to plan several essays in the time it takes to put one together.

8   **Quantity is not the same as quality.** Remind pupils that it's not a matter of writing a lot, rather the matter of writing good quality that counts.

9   **Get pupils to mark essays for themselves.** Sometimes, the best way to alert pupils to the strengths and weaknesses in essay-writing is to help them to allocate marks to examples of essays.

10   **Give pupils the chance to compose an essay as a group.** This can help individual pupils to learn from each other. It can also allow any criticisms to be shared by the group, rather than received by individual pupils.

Chapter 5 Providing personal and pastoral care

The teacher's job does not finish when the end of lesson bell rings. For many, the pastoral elements of our work tend to be some of the most satisfying and rewarding aspects of our jobs. At the same time, however, this part of our work can be problematic, demanding and exhausting. Sometimes we do not know where to start with pastoral matters and often we do not know where to finish. This section aims to give some guidance on some of the most common issues teachers tend to have to deal with when working on a personal level with children, not only concerned with traumas, but also with the more satisfying task of helping students with preparations for the next phase of their lives.

36

Being an effective Form Tutor

This can be one of the most rewarding of all the aspects of the work of a secondary school teacher. You can really get to know your pupils as individuals and they will relate to you on a much more human level than they may do to their subject teachers. Schools vary in the amount of emphasis given to the pastoral role of the Form Tutor but in most cases you will be expected to get to know your group very well and follow their progress on every level.

1   **Get to know your form as individuals.** Learn their names as quickly as you can. Talk to some pupils each day about some aspect of their school or home life. Try not to always talk to the approachable members of the class. Make an effort to involve all the group in activities.

2   **Build a collection of 'portraits' of the pupils in your form.** This can be done with the pupils themselves, for example containing details of their hobbies, favourite foods, best-liked music, sports achievements, and so on. Try to build up a way of finding out what makes each individual 'tick'.

3   **Be an ally, as well as a teacher.** Make it clear to pupils in your form that you are there to help them. This in turn means that you expect them to tell you when they need your help. Be ready to be their principal contact if they need to share personal or family problems that could be affecting their lives.

4   **Praise good social behaviour.** While such behaviour affects all teachers and pupils, it is often left to the Form Tutor to be the monitor of general attitudes and demeanour. Invoke 'team spirit' and a feel of belonging – 'we are the best class' feeling.

5   **Be approachable** – leave time to talk to your class – don't always be preoccupied with administrative tasks or preparing the next lesson.

6   **Be a trouble-shooter!** Offer to help to 'smooth the waves' when pupils in your form get into difficulties with your colleagues. You will often be able to explain to your colleagues difficulties that the particular pupils are going through, that they could not otherwise have known about.

7   **In form base time, set small tasks which will get pupils working together in different configurations.** This helps to avoid the class becoming polarized into cliques that always work together. You can make a number of different sorts of groupings, including alphabetical ones, astrological ones (birthday month), last-letter-of-first-name groups, and so on.

8   **Encourage pride in the form base classroom where feasible.** Providing (or encouraging pupils to provide) posters and plants can help make a form classroom special to the form.

9   **Pay attention to small details.** Some pupils like it when you remember their birthdays or if you comment on their contributions to school exhibitions, performances or sports event achievements.

10 **Recognize individual differences.** You can treat pupils equally without treating them identically. Try to ensure that both genders get equal amounts of time and attention, but don't ignore quiet pupils just because they are no bother.

37

Getting pupils to talk to you

When pupils are talking to you, you have their undivided attention. The more you can get them to do the talking, the more learning they will achieve.

1 **Invite questions from individual pupils by name.** Give them the chance to explain more about their questions, so that everyone becomes interested in the answers.

2 **Make full use of questions pupils ask.** Ask the class if anyone is willing or able to answer a question which a pupil has asked. Give volunteers every encouragement to answer.

3 **Don't 'put down' incorrect answers from pupils.** Gently confirm that the answers are not yet quite correct, and invite further replies from any pupils who have further ideas.

4 **Ask questions in an interesting way.** Make it appear that you really don't yet know what the answers may be. Draw the answers out of pupils, by asking them leading questions, which help them to arrive at sensible answers.

5 **Encourage pupils to contribute their own questions.** Help pupils themselves to think of the questions that the class needs to address. If the class 'owns' the questions, more pupils will be interested in the answers to them.

6 **Be available as an expert witness.** Arrange one-to-one times, where any pupil can come to you, and ask you anything, or tell you anything. Use what they ask or tell you as an agenda for future class discussions or activities.

7 **Be someone who can find someone who knows.** Make it clear to pupils that they can ask you (or tell you) about anything at all, but that you can't be expected to know all the answers – but can find someone who does.

8   **Let pupils in to selected parts of your world.** Talk to classes about 'shareable' things in your own life from time to time, to help the pupils appreciate that you too have feelings and emotions. But handle personal anecdotes with care; it's easy to become boring.

9   **Accept silly questions.** When pupils ask 'silly' questions, or say 'silly' things, treat them as perfectly reasonable questions or comments, encouraging other pupils to ask questions or make comments.

10 **Bring everyone in.** Identify those pupils that don't ask questions or give comments, and try to draw them in to discussions, for example by giving them the responsibility for taking charge of a group-discussion of a matter arising from a question that has already been asked.

38

Helping pupils who don't believe in themselves

Personal self-esteem is important for everyone (including ourselves). Human nature being what it is, there will always be a proportion of pupils who (sometimes for very complex reasons) underestimate themselves. Don't think that you can solve the world's problems by yourself! You'll have too many of your own at first. You may wish to concentrate on teaching and surviving yourself in the early stages! However, some suggestions on how to help pupils with low self-esteem are given below.

1   **Capitalize on their successes.** Remind yourself about how self-belief usually comes through success. Try to ensure that pupils who have a self-esteem problem are given things to do that they will succeed demonstrably in. It can help to break something up into short manageable tasks where such pupils can succeed, before going on to the next stage.

2   **Be aware of sensitivity when giving feedback.** Take particular care when giving feedback to pupils who may be sensitive because of a self-esteem problem. Avoid the use of any negative 'final language' including such words as 'not satisfactory', or 'wrong'.

3   **Help pupils identify their strengths.** Help pupils who are feeling low on self-esteem by reminding them about things that you already know they are good at, and where you can point to evidence which convinces themselves of their achievements.

4   **Help pupils accept their weaknesses.** Encourage pupils to regard weaknesses as not-yet-developed strengths. Help them to believe that the fact that they can't *yet* do a thing does not mean they can never do it.

5   **Show that weaknesses are really opportunities to grow.** Suggest that pupils regard weaknesses as opportunities rather than threats. Show them that being aware of a weakness is in itself a strength, and a cause for positive self-esteem.

6   **Suggest that low-self-esteem is part of life at that time.** Remind pupils that most people go through periods of low self-esteem as a perfectly normal and natural part of growing up and developing. Where possible, give illustrations of your own feelings and approaches during such times.

7   **Help pupils find out what makes them tick.** Do a group exercise with pupils asking 'What sorts of things make you feel good about yourself?'. Several pupils may discover positive factors about themselves that they had not consciously thought about before.

8   **Help pupils to share feelings.** Encourage pupils to go public with (at least some of) their feelings. This will need handling with sensitivity and tact. For example, have a 'feelings washing line' at the side of a classroom, where pupils can peg a piece of paper saying how they feel today and why.

9   **Devise tasks where pupils will succeed.** Have a stock of small useful tasks you can give out to pupils who need a boost in their self-esteem – tasks which you know they can succeed at, and which will be seen by others to have been useful and successful.

10 **Don't forget your own feelings.** Monitor your own self-esteem, and the contributing factors and circumstances. We never stop learning about how our own minds and emotions function.

39

Coping with emotional pupils

Human beings are an emotional species. By the time we become teachers, we've had a fair amount of experience at handling our own emotions. Pupils, however, will continue to meet emotions quite new to them. The following are some of the ways we can help them.

1   **Accept the emotion** – don't try to persuade pupils to 'pull yourself together now!' There may be times when pupils have so much on their minds because of outside circumstances that they are not able to learn. Be sensitive to this and reduce the pressure or discover if they can be helped through it.

2   **Find out what's behind the emotion.** Gently and carefully gather information on the cause of strong emotions. The first explanations of the cause are often far from the real cause. Yawning and lack of concentration may sometimes be outward signs of inward confusion and distress, not boredom with what you are teaching.

3   **Help pupils put it in their own words.** Encourage pupils to explain how they feel, and why they feel that way. Use questions which help to draw out their feelings, without making judgmental replies at any early stage.

4   **Avoid alienating pupils affected by emotion.** Try to avoid the isolation of any pupil experiencing a strong emotion. Help them to feel that emotions are a perfectly normal part of life, and that there is no shame or weakness involved in having emotions.

5   **Help pupils identify the source of their emotions.** When the emotion concerned is anger, help pupils to clarify the exact causes of such feelings. Often, once the causes have been expressed to someone else, the feelings are considerably relieved.

6 **Help pupils see that emotions are natural.** Openly discuss at 'normal' times the human nature of having emotions and feelings. Explain to pupils how the first time they experience particular emotions and feelings, they can feel quite out of their depth, but that subsequent experience helps them develop their own coping strategies.

7 **Don't go it alone.** Don't expect to be able to deal with all emotional situations on your own. Find out which colleagues are particularly good at dealing with such situations, and bring them in when possible to help you.

8 **Bring in the experts when necessary.** Be on the lookout for emotional problems which will benefit from expert help. When following up such expertise, be careful that no feelings of stigma arise. It is often the sensitive and intelligent mind that ties itself in knots temporarily due to over-emotion.

9 **Minimize feelings of weakness.** Do anything you can to minimize the feeling of an over-emotional pupil of 'being different'. Feelings of alienation are often the most distressing part of an emotional episode.

10 **Show that you too are human.** When it is useful, share your own emotions and feelings, and your own ways of coping with swings of mood. Use your judgement to decide which parts of your own experience can be useful for your pupils to learn from.

40

Breaking bad news

Sadly, bad news has to be broken by someone, and that sometimes means us! There is no substitute for a course in counselling, but the following suggestions may provide some ideas about how to break bad news to pupils.

1   **Be sure of your facts.** Make sure you know exactly what the bad news is, and where the information came from. Have contact telephone numbers written down.

2   **Don't do it alone.** If possible, enlist the help of a colleague before you start the difficult task of breaking bad news to a pupil – preferably, a colleague of the opposite sex to yourself.

3   **Prepare the way** – find a suitable location which is private but informal (breaking some bad news in front of a whole class could be very traumatic for the recipient of the news).

4   **Be ready for the next steps.** Plan in advance what will be done after breaking the news (for example who will take the pupil to the hospital, or home).

5   **Avoid highlighting bad news.** Call the pupil concerned out of the class as innocently as possible (for example 'Sorry, but could we go along to Mrs Roger's room where I believe she has a message for you?').

6   **Proceed gently.** If possible, invite the pupil to sit down first. Only then say something along the lines 'I'm sorry, but I've got some rather bad news for you' then deliver the news as gently as possible, giving what comfort you can as needed.

7   **Accept emotional reactions.** If the news results in tears, it is usually best to encourage 'that's all right now, let it all out' rather than say 'pull yourself together'! Particularly when you've a colleague present, one or other of you can hold a hand or give a hug as appropriate.

8   **Inform other people with due care.** It may be necessary to tell the rest of the class about the bad news. However, it's important not to break confidences at this stage. For example, it's better to tell them that 'Sheila has had some sad news which will have given her a bit of a shock' rather than to say 'Sheila's mother has been injured in an accident'.

9   **Decide who needs to know what.** Depending on the nature of the news, decide whether all of your colleagues need to be alerted to the details, or just the fact that the pupil concerned needs to be treated with particular sensitivity during the time to come.

10   **Keep track of events.** It can make a big difference if you can continue to monitor the situation. This may mean maintaining contact with the pupil or the family, in which case it is important that one person does this rather than too many callers or enquirers.

41

Helping pupils to recover from setbacks

Sometimes circumstances overtake all of us. Pupils may lose a fortnight due to illness, or have setbacks in their family lives which knock them out of their stride. Also, pupils often need help in recovering from failure. The following suggestions may help you to help them to regain their momentum.

1   **Assemble your first-aid kit.** Build up your own collection of handouts and resources covering key topics in your teaching which you can issue to pupils. This can help you to assist pupils to make up for lost time when necessary.

2   **Encourage pupils to ask.** Encourage pupils who have missed key lessons on important topics to make lists of questions about things they can't understand as they work on catching up. Make time to be available to respond to these questions.

3   **Encourage peer-group support.** Help pupils who have missed something to use their classmates as a resource to help them catch up. Explain to the whole class how useful it is to explain a topic to someone.

4   **Don't look back yet!** Suggest to pupils who have fallen behind that it is more important to keep up with what is going on at present than to try and do all the catching up overnight. Encourage them to catch up a bit at a time, while keeping up with the rest of the class on current topics as well.

5   **Have other ways of catching up ready.** For particularly crucial parts of your course, have alternative learning pathways readily available for any pupils who miss key lessons. For example, turn these parts into small learning packages or interactive handouts, which pupils can work through in their own time. Also, run 'repeat' (rather than 'remedial') sessions on these key topics, for anyone who did not 'get it' first time round.

6   **Help pupils not to panic.** Help pupils who have missed something important to keep it in perspective. It may seem like a mountain at the time, but once understood, the problem will be forgotten quickly.

7   **Encourage pupils to regard 'failure' as a useful stage towards success.** Remind them that they themselves are not failures; it is simply that they have not yet succeeded at the particular task involved.

8   **Acknowledge the value of making mistakes.** Give pupils examples of how 'getting it wrong at first' is one of the most natural ways to learn things successfully.

9   **Help pupils look at their tactics.** Where pupils are preparing for a re-sit exam, encourage them not only to explore the parts that caused them problems before, but also to analyse they ways they went about preparing for the exam and sitting it. Indeed, advise pupils that a past failure can be a distinct advantage when it comes to the next occasion.

10 **Tell them about Edison,** whose 100th attempt to make an electric light bulb was successful. He dismissed the rest as '99 ways *not* to try to make a light bulb'.

42

Helping pupils towards university or employment

Sometimes, it is thought that the 'Careers Advisor' bears all the responsibility for the future progress of pupils. However, pupils need all the guidance and support we can all give them in addition to specialist advice. The following suggestions may help you to support your own pupils.

1   **Help pupils make their own resources.** Ask pupils to prepare a 'Curriculum Vitae' as an assessed task. Give them feedback on the ways that their CVs may be viewed by Admission Tutors in universities, or by prospective employers.

2   **Help pupils fly their own kites.** Help pupils to identify strengths in their own experience, which are worth showing clearly when they apply for employment or further education.

3   **Show pupils what counts.** Alert pupils to the things that look 'good' on applications. In particular, extol the virtues of things that show pupils' responsibility, cooperativeness, and initiative.

4   **Coach pupils in the art of 'interview technique'.** Use class role-play exercises to help pupils familiarize themselves with the processes of interviews.

5   **Give pupils safe 'dry-runs'.** If possible, engage pupils in making videos of simulated interviews. Remember that the act of capturing on video an interview automatically develops quite acute observation of the processes involved.

6   **Help pupils see what's being sought.** Use case-studies to alert pupils to what prospective interviewers may be looking for. For example, show pupils a video of three different interviews for a job, and ask them to list the respective merits and weaknesses of the candidates, and to select the best candidate.

7   **Let pupils taste further opportunities.** Take advantage of open days at local colleges or universities, to give pupils a taste of what it would be like to continue their education there.

8   **Help pupils see what has already succeeded.** Invite past pupils who gained employment or went on to college back to the school to share their experience with pupils.

9   **Help pupils find out what they need to be able to do.** Set groups of pupils the task of drawing up an advertisement for a job, spelling out the duties involved in the job, and identifying the experience that is being sought in candidates.

10   **Practice makes perfect.** Remind pupils that becoming good at interviews is best achieved by practice, and that one 'bad' interview should not put them off. Encourage them to learn even more from unsuccessful interviews than from successful ones.

43

Coping with parents' evenings

These occasions can prove quite an ordeal at the end of a busy day – especially if you're not well prepared. In some subject areas you could come into contact with 250 different pupils each week so if you can get into the habit of writing brief notes about pupils' progress as it happens, you will find interviews with parents much less worrying. Parents evenings are not the place to discuss major issues, and if possible you should let parents know in advance if there are serious matters which may need lengthier or more private discussions. As a general rule, there should be no major surprises in store for parents.

1   **Establish which parents will be attending.** Talk to your pupils in advance, and tune in to how they feel about parental visits to the school. Discuss with the pupils what they feel their successes and failures have been so far in the course.

2   **Make it clear to parents who you are.** This is particularly important when parents' evenings are held in a large space such as the School Hall. Have a large card on your table, with your name on it and the subject you teach, or the form you are responsible for.

3   **Make sure you know who the pupils are!** If it is too early in the term to have learnt all their names, ensure that you check out your notes and marks when the class is present during lessons beforehand. Make very brief notes about any individual achievements or characteristics in your mark book as you become aware of them. This will be an invaluable aid to writing reports later in the term.

4   **Take along some examples of the pupil's work where appropriate.** Parents are very interested not only in their own child's progress but also in the type of work done in lessons.

5   **Make brief notes of which parents talk to you, and the main points of discussion.** You will often want to follow up particular things arising from the discussion later.

6   **Avoid odious comparisons.** Talk about the pupil under consideration, rather than their classmates or siblings. When such comparisons are indulged in, it can be surprising how far the teacher's words will be reported, and how long the memory can be retained.

7   **Look after yourself.** Try to arrange for a hot drink to be brought to you, or at least have in reserve mineral water and mints. These evenings can be very long.

8   **Concentrate on pupils' behaviour and achievements rather than personality issues.** Parents may be more amenable to criticisms of what their children are actually doing rather than their children's personality traits (which may be inherited!).

9   **Avoid the temptation to get drawn into discussions of the shortcomings of other members of staff.** However justified and satisfying this may sometimes be, it is not terribly professional!

10   **Try not to speed up towards the end!** You may be tired, but the last parents to see you may well have been waiting a long time, and they deserve just as much of your attention as those you saw at the beginning of the evening.

44

Dealing with difficult parents

Difficult parents usually are ones who come to complain! The best advice to offer is not to deal directly with difficult parents – but get someone who is paid to do that sort of job to handle it. This does not always work out so easily in practice. The following suggestions may help you when it falls to you to sort out a difficult situation. The first two suggestions are evasion tactics – but you'll need the rest sooner or later too!

1 **Refer the complaint to your Head of Department**. Alternatively, refer it to a more senior member of staff and if possible get them to deal with it without involving you in face-to-face contact with the parents. (Perhaps you should also pass on to your senior colleague a copy of this list!)

2 **If you have made a mistake, admit it.** Report it factually to your Head of Department or Headteacher and let them sort it out on your behalf.

3 **Develop your listening skills!** The cause of many difficult encounters is that parents don't feel that we are letting them tell us what is concerning them. It is all too easy to jump in far too early to try to defend ourselves. Let them have their full say – indeed, draw their concerns from them. Then prepare to reply.

4 **Think of difficulties in terms of situations and actions, rather than people.** Explain to parents (and pupils) that it has nothing to do with particular personalities, but is a matter of events, consequences and effects.

5 **Avoid difficulties 'spilling over'.** When you have had a difficulty with a pupil (or a parent) over one matter, make it clear that this does not cause you to bear a grudge, and that you are treating every new situation as a fresh start.

6 **Rehearse the rationale of your own position.** Before you discuss any matters concerning their child with parents, make sure that you are clear in your own mind of the reasons for your actions and behaviour. If they can see your point of view, they are likely to become less difficult.

7 **Stay calm, don't get drawn into arguments.** Repeat your own version of events and justify it in a professional manner. Avoid confrontation – know when you can back down discreetly and when it is important not to. When you suspect that there could be major difficulties, ensure that you don't see parents completely on your own.

8 **Be prepared to understand, even when you don't agree.** Often, difficulties can be caused when parents can't see that you understand their point of view. If you can convince them that you do indeed understand, but in your professional capacity can't agree with them, they may become more ready to listen to your own point of view.

9 **Be the first to re-build bridges.** This sometimes goes against human nature, but we teachers as professional people are often better able to re-open channels of communication after a difficulty.

10 **Use encounters with difficult parents as a learning opportunity.** Painful as it may be at the time, we can build up a lot of experience by learning from each encounter, and asking ourselves 'what would I do differently if a similar situation arises tomorrow?'.

45

Coping with emergencies

We can forgive ourselves for having nightmares about emergencies and how we may cope with them! However, an important part of the learning experience of our pupils is seeing how we cope with the unexpected. The following suggestions may help you rise to the occasion when necessary.

1   **Look positively at emergencies.** Remind yourself that each emergency you are faced with is a productive learning experience, and that next time a similar situation arises, you will have your additional experience to help you out.

2   **Be prepared.** Anticipate as many emergencies as is reasonable to expect. For example, get some training in first-aid. Being that bit more confident can make a lot of difference to how you feel when coping with a crisis.

3   **Expect the unexpected!** 'Emergencies' are by definition 'the unexpected'. Take positive steps to be alert to early-warning signals, so that nothing is really unexpected.

4   **Know someone who's good at dealing with the unexpected.** Build your own support network of people who are good at handling difficult or stressful situations. Learn from them, observing their coping strategies.

5   **Don't try to do all the coping on your own.** Other pupils may be able to do useful things to help you to focus your own efforts on the most critical parts of the actions needed to handle an emergency.

6   **Move the emergency.** When possible, take the emergency to a less public place. A quiet corner of an empty classroom may be better territory to sort out an emergency than in front of a whole class.

7   **No-one can handle all emergencies first time.** Don't expect that you are required to cope with distinction with each and every emergency you ever meet. When things don't work out, don't dwell on feelings of failure, but rather extract what you can learn from the situation, then let it go.

8   **Collect case lore.** With colleagues, build up a collection of case-study notes on emergencies and how they were handled. Learn from things that succeeded in the past, and also from things that could have been handled more successfully with hindsight.

9   **Be ready to act.** Be as prepared as you can. For example, have quick access to pupils' home addresses and telephone numbers, and ensure that you keep your personal datafile updated and close to hand.

10   **Don't panic!** Being seen to panic helps no-one. Try to appear calm and collected even when your mind is in a whirl! Remind yourself that emergencies are usually over in a very short time – it only *seems* like a century.

Chapter 6   Being an effective colleague

A commonly overheard remark in the staff room is 'I can cope with the kids, it's the other teachers that are driving me up the wall!' This short section offers some advice on how to work effectively with fellow professionals within the school, how to take care of yourself and some thoughts on looking to your own future.

46

Working with colleagues

It can be lonely at the chalkface! Yet it does often carry the comfort of privacy. However, with cross-curriculum developments and initiatives, it is becoming increasingly important for teachers to be able to work together effectively and constructively. There are many benefits to be realized from collaborative working, not least the fact that colleagues can take over from us at short notice when necessary. It also helps to feel you have friends and allies when the going gets tough. The following suggestions may help you to take advantage of such benefits.

1   **Collaborate with colleagues.** Co-produce with colleagues teaching and learning materials as much as possible to produce co-ownership of resources. The quality and effectiveness of resources produced by more than one teacher are much higher than we could have produced on our own (your three co-authors have found this in writing this book together!).

2   **Keep colleagues well informed.** Brief colleagues working with you carefully, especially any part-time colleagues or temporary teachers who could not be with you during planning discussions for the courses you're teaching. Keep colleagues informed about how your own work is going too.

3   **Plan how you will work jointly.** Plan and organize your collaborative work well in advance, for example, using flowcharts to show how your roles will integrate.

4   **Plan to be able to cover for each other.** Develop your ability to provide emergency backup for other colleagues to cope with contingencies. Help colleagues to be able to take over from you at short notice when necessary too.

5   **All work and no play?** Take full advantage of social opportunities to get to know colleagues informally, so you can enjoy each other's company out of the context of your work as well as in school.

6   **Don't be seen to disagree!** Ensure that when your views or opinions differ with those of colleagues, you avoid arguing in the presence of pupils! And if you are new to teaching, don't forget you may have a lot to learn from older hands.

7   **Keep to deadlines.** Meet deadlines for collaborative tasks when colleagues are relying on you keeping to schedules on time. Attend meetings promptly and properly prepared.

8   **Share your own resources and skills.** Make available to colleagues your teaching materials, including overheads, handouts, and exercises. Invite colleagues to observe or participate in some of your lessons, and ask for their comments about how the sessions went. Similarly, respond to colleagues' invitations or requests to sit in on their lessons, and give them feedback kindly and supportively when they request it.

9   **Be willing to ask for help.** Seek advice and suggestions from colleagues (even when you don't need it) and make your colleagues feel valued and respected for their help.

10   **Monitor collaborative working.** Promote the benefits of team teaching to colleagues, and help them start to work in teams. Take time to review openly the processes by which you work together, and improve and develop these processes whenever you can.

47

Coping with difficult Heads of Department or senior staff

If you are finding one of your superiors difficult to deal with, the chances are you are not the only one. Find an ally and discuss the problem in confidence – it will give you the strength to carry on!

1   **Be careful to distinguish between conflicts of ideas and conflicts of personality.** It is possible to work with people in either situation, but easier to manage when you know exactly what sorts of conflict are involved.

2   **Refrain from inappropriately aggressive behaviour in conflict situations.** This includes consciously refraining from sarcasm, cynical remarks and bursts of temper.

3   **Find out what other colleagues think too.** Get other colleagues to witness your achievements as well as your boss. Enlist the support of others in your department and work together as a team.

4   **Avoid letting previous differences of opinion colour current interactions.** It is possible to agree on present issues even when you've already disagreed on past matters.

5   **Value other people's opinions, even when they are the opposite of your own.** You can disagree completely with what someone thinks about an issue, without taking away their right to have their own views.

6   **Avoid the temptation to undermine the professional dignity of self-esteem of 'difficult' senior colleagues.** They will usually be in a position to return such actions doubly!

7   **Check that you are indeed trying to do what senior colleagues ask you to do.** Make a note of what you have been asked to do and check this with a senior teacher before and after completion.

8   **Identify the exact nature of a difficulty.** Talk about it to senior members of staff on a professional level ensuring that others understand your situation. Try to develop a simple action plan to help you overcome the difficulty.

9   **Cover your tracks.** Ensure that difficulties are placed on the agenda for department meetings, and that decisions are minuted – offer to take the minutes yourself if necessary.

10   **Accept that it's not easy being the boss!** There may be all kinds of pressures, of which you are quite unaware, on your Head of Department.

48
Managing a department

Although you may not yet be in the position of Head of Department, it is useful to be aware of the issues involved in such responsibilities, and the difficulties that might arise. Of course, if you're brave enough, you may decide to copy the suggestions below to your Head of Department (anonymously!!).

1   **Hold regular meetings with staff, which are timetabled in advance.** This ensures that everyone is ready to attend, even if there is little on the agenda. You can always cancel a meeting if there is nothing to discuss, but it is sometimes difficult to get colleagues together at short notice when there is something important to decide. Regular meetings, even if only brief, ease communication and foster a sense of belonging to a team.

2   **Meetings should always have an agenda and be minuted.** Don't prolong meetings unnecessarily – prioritize items of business and set time limits for discussion if there is a lot on the agenda. Adopt the philosophy that a well-chaired one-hour meeting can always cover as much ground as a half-day meeting!

3   **Get members of the department to take the minutes in rotation**. The act of minuting a meeting helps people to distance themselves at least temporarily from their own personal points of view, and overall helps to keep things in perspective.

4   **Make the outcomes of meetings definite and accessible.** Ensure that things which must be done are put in writing and accompanied by a completion date, and that all colleagues receive them.

5   **Delegate areas of responsibility fairly within the department.** Ensure that new or inexperienced colleagues also take some area of responsibility however small.

6   **Ensure that all staff feel valued and involved.** Involve all colleagues in discussions of the allocation of capitation, and in budgeting and ordering of stock.

7   **Adopt a team approach to planning.** Get colleagues to work together to develop policies so that all are involved at every stage. When everyone in the Department has a sense of ownership of plans and policies, it is more likely that the plans will come to fruition smoothly and quickly.

8   **Keep everyone fully informed, but minimize paperwork.** Avoid excessive use of circulated papers and memoranda. These may move swiftly from pigeonhole to wastepaper basket! Use a notice board which all can access to aid communication. Have space on the board for individual colleagues to post replies or reactions to decisions, so that all views can be shared.

9   **Plan social as well as business meetings for the department.** When people are friends as well as colleagues, a Department runs happily.

10   **Acknowledge difficult decisions.** When a decision needs to be taken, on a matter where there are different opinions, facilitate a group session where staff can express the strengths and weaknesses they see in various alternative approaches to the decision to be made. If there is no clear outcome, agree on a trial approach, with a review date when the matter will be discussed on the basis of experience of the trial.

49

Covering for absent colleagues

'Oh but I'm indispensable!' wouldn't we all like to think? That fact is that now and again someone is going to have to take over for us, and sometimes at very short notice indeed. Similarly, we need to be able to cover for absent colleagues. The following suggestions may help you make your 'guest appearances' successful – and less stressful for you.

1   **If possible, get an oral briefing in advance.** When colleagues are taking planned absence, this helps so you can clarify exactly what you are required to do.

2   **Try to have available an assortment of activities for all ages and abilities.** This can prove invaluable when you are left in the lurch without work set for pupils to do. Such activities might include crosswords, word-searches, reading tasks, puzzles, and discussion topics.

3   **Carry with you an emergency pack of paper, ballpoint pens, and so on, for pupils to use.** Absent teachers often have the set of exercise books at home with them, especially if it is an unexpected absence.

4   **Don't expect to be able to learn names in a one-off substitution class.** However, it may be helpful to draw a sketch plan of the desk positions and pass it round at the beginning of the class, asking pupils to write in their names (legibly). This may help you to identify pupils and to have a class register (but be aware that some might take the mickey out of you by substituting false names!).

5   **Don't allow yourself to get drawn into discussions about how much better you are than their normal teacher!** This may be flattering, but doesn't engender a professional and collegial approach.

6   **Don't be over-ambitious about what you can achieve.** Especially with a one-off substitution, be realistic about what you are likely to be able to do as a relative stranger to the pupils.

7   **Don't stand for any nonsense.** Use all the techniques in your repertoire to settle pupils down and maintain order. Remember that pupils will often try to give cover teachers a hard time!

8   **Don't be surprised if pupils are angry or resentful about you covering their class.** Some pupils hate change, and you may be replacing their favourite teacher.

9   **Keep your sense of humour.** This may be difficult in trying circumstances, but do your best!

10   **Be considerate to the absent teacher.** Ensure that pupils leave the room tidy, and count in all materials used. Coming back to depleted stock after an illness or emergency is not encouraging!

50

Coping with stress

Our job can be a stressful one. In addition, there are episodes of stress in most people's lives at one time or another. The following suggestions may help you to handle stressful times.

1 **Accept that stress is a natural part of human life.** Accept also that it does not help at all simply to allocate blame for our feelings of stress, or to rail against the situation. It is more useful to find ways of coping with stress, than to expend energy on wishing that it was not there.

2 **Regard stress as useful!** Try to develop the attitude that every stressful situation can be viewed as a useful developmental experience. Learning to cope with stress, or even 'going under' temporarily, can both be used to build up coping strategies.

3 **Monitor your stress levels.** Keep track of whether you are stressed or not – you may not realize it when you are in fact stressed. Other people can often tell us about our stress levels – provided we give them the chance and don't shout them down!

4 **Decide when stress needs some action.** Accept that a certain amount of stress is actually healthy, raising our adrenalin levels and creative thinking capacities. The time to worry about stress is when it gets in the way of a balanced, enjoyable life, or affects people around us.

5 **Be aware of the symptoms of stress.** Remember that when we are stressed, we can easily magnify small irritations out of all proportions. If you find yourself overreacting to everyday things pupils do, don't blame them, it may be *you* getting things out of proportion.

6 **Build up your own support network.** Include family, friends, colleagues and even relative strangers. Getting away from a stressful situation for a while can help us to recharge our batteries and return better able to handle it.

7   **Exchange with colleagues and friends strategies for coping with stress.** It is most productive to do this at a time when you feel quite unstressed, as you can then look at the various coping strategies calmly and objectively.

8   **It's up to us how we react to stress.** Common as it is for other people to get the blame for our stress, there's little anyone can do to alter how other people are, or how they behave. It is our task to readjust our reactions to stressful situation.

9   **Many kinds of stress are completely avoidable.** These include the stress we may feel when we're late, or unprepared. But remember it is sometimes possible simply to say 'No!'.

10   **Don't cross too many bridges!** One of the biggest stress factors we have to cope with is the possibility of failure or rejection. It is human nature to worry about many things that simply don't ever happen. Save your mental energies for handling the few things that need your coping strategies.

51

Planning your career progression

When you start out in teaching it may seem a miracle to you that you have managed to survive your first year without having a nervous breakdown or getting the sack! It can, however, be surprising how soon the opportunity may come up to develop your skills and further your career. INSET (In-Service Education and Training) opportunities can play a vital part in extending the range of teaching that you can handle well.

1   **Attend INSET wherever possible,** if at all relevant to your work. You could end up as the only person around with some specialist knowledge. The more things you know at least a bit about, the greater your employability.

2   **The best way to learn is to try to teach!** Make the most of every opportunity to run INSET workshops or discussions within your department or school in your own specialist area. However, if you are new to teaching, don't try to teach any grandparent to suck eggs!

3   **Keep yourself informed.** Take an interest in wider educational issues; read the educational press and attend professional association meetings.

4   **Set yourself clear goals** – even if they seem unrealistic to start with. Where do you want to be in five years' time, and what would it take to get you there? Use the appraisal process to help you clarify and plan your personal and professional development.

5   **Cultivate your profile.** Make sure that people know what you are doing in the classroom, and if you are involved in any initiatives, pilot schemes, and developments.

6   **Involve yourself in extra-curricular activities.** Use your outside interests and hobbies to extend your contribution to the full range of things that the school offers pupils and staff.

7   **Take opportunities to work-shadow other colleagues.** One of the most productive ways of improving one's own teaching is to see how other people do it well – and better still, how they do it badly!

8   **Build up your own network.** Take every opportunity to make contacts with teachers involved in your subject in other schools. Exchange ideas, and teaching and learning resources with them.

9   **Keep on studying.** Always be on the lookout for ways you can extend the subject range which one day you may wish to teach.

10   **Build up your own teaching portfolio.** Keep a collection of things you have designed, reflections on new ideas you have tried out. Such a portfolio can be very valuable when it comes to appraisal interviews, or interviews for promotion or new posts elsewhere. It's often a good idea to keep a collection of photographs of activities and events you've organized or planned which might otherwise be difficult to document.

52

Applying for jobs

In most professions including teaching, advancement nowadays more often seems to come through moving on than by staying put. The following suggestions may help you move on when you want to.

1 **Keep up your Curriculum Vitae as an on-going task** – preferably on computer disc. It is extremely useful to be able to print off an updated copy at short notice, when an interesting opportunity seems worth applying for.

2 **Make your CV read interestingly** – not just a catalogue of all the things you've done in your career. If people find your CV interesting to read, they are likely to be keener to find out more about you, and your chance of being shortlisted for a job is increased.

3 **Get your wording right.** Take care in working out the wording you will use in a convincing letter of application for a post. Make such letters specific to the school and the post that you are applying for, and include indications of how you personally would approach taking on the post.

4 **Keep up appearances.** Remember how important the appearance of a completed application form can be. It is often difficult to type in information into boxes on printed forms, so decide whether to engage a skilled typist, or to practise yourself on photocopies of the form until you can get it just right.

5 **Know what you said to whom.** Especially when you may have several applications in progress at one time, it is essential to keep photocopies of exactly what you said in each particular instance. The exact words you used make ideal reading while preparing for any interview you're called to – it is the self-same words which are being read by the interview panel.

6   **Remember the importance of face-to-face communication skills.** If you are to convince other people at interviews, these skills will be valuable to you. Face-to-face skills at an interview are of course taken as an indicator of how you can work with pupils too.

7   **Be prepared for open-ended questions.** Often, at an interview you will be asked to 'tell us a bit about yourself'. Such questions can be harder to handle than direct questions about your experience. Practise giving (say) a three-minute summary of your career to date, focusing on your successes rather than any difficulties you've met.

8   **All interviews are useful experiences – even the painful ones.** Regard each interview not as the one-and-only opportunity to the job of your dreams, but as a useful chance to develop and improve your approach in the future. It's often when you don't particularly want the job in question that you're offered the most interesting options!

9   **Practice helps a lot!** If you can make the chance, practise your interview technique with friends or colleagues. It's good for any of us to become used to the sound or our own voices answering questions and talking about our aims and ambitions.

10   **Don't let your technique go rusty!** Apply for new jobs regularly anyway, even when you're perfectly satisfied with your present post. It is always useful experience to take stock of your career to date, and it is often valuable to show your colleagues that you're not necessarily content with your present status. 'Nothing ventured, nothing gained' is a useful motto!

Chapter 7   Information and communications technologies

Since we wrote the first edition of this book, the use of information and communication technologies in schools (and throughout society in the developed world) has expanded faster than most people would have imagined possible. We end this book with a selection of suggestions about using various computer-based and electronic means to help your pupils to learn effectively and enjoyably. We have also included in this chapter some suggestions relating to simpler media such as video and audiotape, as to use these for effective learning, similar considerations need to be put into practice as when using the most sophisticated of the information and communications technologies – in particular, keeping the intended learning outcomes firmly in view, and making sure that pupils learn actively from each medium.

We hope that the suggestions in this chapter will help you to bring your pupils into the modern world of information technology. We also hope that these suggestions will help *you* to find out more about any of these technology dimensions with which you are not already familiar.

53

Choosing computer-aided learning packages

Computer-based packages are widely used in schools, and also play a valuable part in open learning programmes, and indeed have largely been developed for the open learning market. As open or flexible learning pathways are used more widely within school provision, the range of computer-based learning resources continues to grow rapidly. There may well be computer-based packages which will be helpful to your own pupils. The following suggestions can provide help in selecting computer-aided learning packages for your pupils.

1 **Remember that it's harder to get a good idea of the effectiveness of computer-based materials than for paper-based ones.** This is not least because it is not possible to flick through the whole of a computer-based package in the same way as is possible with a printed package. It can be quite hard to get a feel for the overall shape of the learning that is intended to accompany a computer-based package.

2 **Choose your packages carefully.** The best computer-based learning packages are not always those which look most attractive, nor are they necessarily the most expensive ones. The best indicator of a good package is evidence that they cause learning to be successful. Where possible, try them out on pupils before committing your school to purchasing them. Alternatively, ask the supplier or manufacturer for details of clients who have already used the packages, and check that the packages really deliver what you need.

3 **Prepare your own checklist to interrogate computer-based materials.** Decide the questions that you need to ask about each possible package. Questions could include:

   • Are the materials supplied with workbook elements?

   • Do pupils themselves *need* these elements?

- Can support materials be freely photocopied?
- What is the standard of the equipment needed to run the packages effectively?
- What level of technical support and backup will be required?
- Is this available within your school?
- Does the software include individual pupil progress monitoring and tracking?
- Do the materials make good use of pre-test and post-test features?
- Can the materials run effectively on a network?
- Are there licensing implications if you wish to run the package on more than one machine?
- Can you afford multiple copies if the materials are multimedia, single-access packages?

4   **Try to establish the pedigree of the software.** Some computer-based packages have been thoroughly tested and developed, and have been updated and revised several times since their launch. Such packages normally give some details of the history of their development. Beware of packages, however well presented, that have been published or disseminated without real trialling.

5   **Find out about packages from colleagues in other schools.** Use your contacts. Ask them what packages they know of, which work well and really help pupils to learn. Also ask them about packages that they don't rate highly, and about the factors that led them to this conclusion.

6   **Try before you buy.** Computer-aided learning packages can be quite expensive, especially if you need to purchase a site licence to use them on a series of networked computer terminals, or to issue pupils with their own copies on floppy disk. If you're considering buying a particular package, try to get a sample of your pupils to evaluate it for you. Their experience of using it is even more valuable than your own, as only they can tell whether they are learning effectively from it.

7   **Look at how the medium is used to enhance learning.** If the material does no more than to present on screen something which could have been presented equally well on paper, it is probably not worth investigating further. The medium should do something that helps learning, such as causing pupils to engage in interaction that they may have skipped if the same tasks or questions were set in print.

8   **Get familiar with the package, before letting your pupils loose with it.**
There is a learning curve to be ascended with most computer-based
packages, and it is best if *you* go up this ahead of your pupils. They will
need help on how to make best use of the package, as well as on what
they are supposed to be learning from it. Find out what it feels like to use
the package. By far the best way to do this is to work through the package
yourself, even if you already know the subject that it covers. Find out
what pupils will *do* as they use the package, and check whether the tasks
and activities are really relevant to your pupils, and pitched at an
appropriate level for them.

9   **Check the intended learning outcomes of the computer-based package.**
The best packages state the intended learning outcomes clearly within
the first few screens of information. Alternatively, the intended outcomes
may be spelled out in supporting documentation which comes with the
package itself. The main danger is that such packages address a wider
range of intended outcomes than are needed by your pupils, and that
they may become distracted and end up learning things that they don't
need to, possibly interfering with their assessment performance.

10   **If necessary, rephrase the learning outcomes associated with the
package.** It may be useful to tell your pupils exactly what the learning
outcomes mean in the context of their particular studies. This will help
them to concentrate on the most important things in the package.

11   **Think about access to equipment and software.** It can be prohibitively
expensive to give each pupil access to the software and the hardware
needed. However, if the package is an important part of their overall
programme, ways need to be found to maximize their opportunity to
work with it. Some packages come with licence arrangements to use the
package with a given number of pupils, or on a whole-school basis, either
allowing multiple copies to be made, or the package to be used over a
network. Ensure that the software is protected in order to prevent
unauthorized copying, or unlicensed use.

12   **Think how pupils will retain important ideas from the package, after
they have used it.** Make sure that there is supporting documentation or
workbook materials, as these will help pupils to summarize and remember
the important things they gain while using computer-based packages.
Where such resources don't already exist, you should consider the benefits
of making a workbook or an interactive handout, so that pupils working
through the package write down things (or record them) at important
stages in their learning.

13 **Ensure that learning-by-doing is appropriate and relevant.** Most computer-based packages contain a considerable amount of learning-by-doing, particularly decision-making, choosing options, and entering responses to structured questions. Some of the tasks may not be entirely relevant to the intended learning outcomes of your course, and you may need to devise briefing details to help pupils to see exactly what they should be taking seriously as they work through the package.

14 **Check that pupils will get adequate feedback on their work with the package.** Much of this feedback may be already built in to the package as it stands. However, you may need to think about further ways of keeping track of whether your pupils are getting what they should from their use of the package. It can be worth adding appropriate, short elements to teacher-marked assignments, so that there is a way of finding out whether particular pupils are missing vital things they should have picked up from the package. One of the main strengths of computer-based learning packages is that pupils can be given instant feedback every time they select an option in a multiple choice question, or key in a word or phrase, and so on. The feedback should be much more than just the correct answer to the question or task. Pupils who get it wrong need to find out from the programme *why* their answer or response was wrong, and exactly *what* was wrong about it.

15 **Check how long the package should take.** The time spent by pupils should be reflected in the learning pay-off they derive from their studies with the package, and this in turn should relate to the proportion of the overall assessment framework that is linked to the topics covered by the package. Many computer-based learning packages come with indications of the expected timescales that are involved in using them, but it is well worth finding out how long typical pupils actually take. Some computer-based packages can make this easier for you by logging the amount of time individuals spend working through them.

16 **Think ahead to assessment.** Work out what will be assessed, relating directly to the learning that is to be done using the computer-based materials. Make sure that pupils, before working through the computer-based materials, know *what* will be assessed, *when* it will be assessed, and *how* it will be assessed.

17 **Explore software that keeps track of pupils' progress.** Many computer-based materials can be used to track individual pupils' progress through them. This can involve pre-testing and post-testing, and storing the data on the computer system, as well as monitoring and recording the time taken by each pupil to work through each part of the package. Such data can be invaluable for discovering the main problems that pupils may be experiencing with the topic, and with the package itself.

18 **Seek feedback from your pupils.** Ask them what aspects of the package they found most valuable, and most important. Ask them also what, if anything, went wrong in their own work with the package. Look in the feedback you obtain for anything that throws light on particular categories of pupils finding difficulties with learning from the package (for example, speakers of other languages, or pupils who are not confident with new technologies). Where possible, find alternative ways of addressing important learning outcomes for those pupils who have particular problems with the computer-delivered materials.

54

Getting pupils used to the idea of learning from a machine

Even though many of your pupils will have a lot of experience of playing with computer-based games, some are likely to believe that they need a human being to teach them, and that they can't learn from mere machines. The following suggestions may help you to win them over, so that they are more receptive to letting computers teach them.

1 **Remind them that there's always a human brain behind the machine.** When necessary, explain to pupils that the computer is merely a vehicle for storing human expertise, and that it's not actually the computer that will be planning what they should learn.

2 **Perhaps tell them that the computer may be better than you are!** In other words, the expertise that will have gone into the computer-designed learning packages is likely to be broader than that of any one person. The people who put together good quality learning packages are normally very experienced in their field, and are likely to be expert teachers in their own right.

3 **Explain that working (as opposed to just playing) with computers is an important life skill.** Gaining confidence and competence with computers is likely to spill over into your pupils' future careers and lives, and will make them more easily updated and retrained as further advances are made in their fields.

4 **Convince your pupils that learning from computers can be great fun.** Once they are over any fear that they will break the equipment, or that the computer will 'think' that they are silly, most people actually take pleasure in getting a computer to work for them.

5   **Remind your pupils of the comfort of making mistakes in privacy.** When pupils get tasks or exercises wrong, in computer-based learning only the computer knows – and computers don't mind! Therefore, it is much better to learn from their mistakes using a computer than when human teachers can see each and every slip.

6   **Point out that when using computers, your pupils don't have to waste time on things they already know.** In class, the whole group is often held up until someone catches up. With computers, anyone who already knows something can press on to something more demanding, without having to wait for anyone to catch up. Computer-aided learning can accommodate pupils' own pace of learning.

7   **Computers don't mind the plea: 'run that by me again'.** Some things are not learned properly first time round. It's not always convenient (or possible) to ask a teacher to go once more through something that a pupil might find difficult, but a computer will go through it as many times as it takes to get the message firmly home.

8   **Remind your pupils that they learn most things by having a go at them.** When they learn-by-doing using a machine, they're being supported every step of the way, and most computer-based packages are highly interactive, and force pupils into making decisions, working things out, selecting the best answers to questions from a range of alternatives, and so on. This means that these aspects of their learning can be much more focused and efficient than in a group learning situation.

9   **Suggest that teachers are there for more important roles.** While pupils can learn things from machines, human beings are better at helping to measure and evaluate their learning, and explaining in other ways any parts which the computer was unable to teach them.

10   **Remind them that they don't have to work alone with computers.** While it may be intended that the computer-based learning materials are for individual use and independent learning, it can be very useful for clusters of pupils to explore together a learning package. This allows them to compare notes on what they find out, and to learn from each other and explain things to each other. This can be a useful first step before setting out to work through a package in depth, independently.

55

Getting pupils used to mice and keyboards

It is increasingly recognized that pupils need to be equipped to function in the world of computers, electronic communication, and the Internet. Most pupils are already highly developed regarding their use of computers from their experience in primary schools or at home. The skills involved all start with them being able to use the basics of all computer-based systems, keyboards and mice. Becoming good at using computers, like most other things, is best learnt by doing it. The following suggestions may help you to make the processes of gaining skill with keyboards and mice more enjoyable and efficient for any of your pupils who have not already picked up skills and speed in primary schools.

1   **Remind your pupils that in most computer operations, not all of the keys need to be used.** The most important keys tend to be the 'enter' key (for commands), the letter keys for text-entry, and the number keys for number-entry or calculations. The function keys may be much more rarely used, especially when first starting to use computers.

2   **Make the most of 'undo' facilities in software.** In many word-processing packages, for example, it is possible to 'undo' a series of keyboard entries. This can be particularly useful when pupils can't remember exactly what they actually did, but know that something has gone wrong. They can also try using the 're-do' command, to find out, step-by-step, what they may have done when something went wrong.

3   **Encourage your pupils to learn to touch-type.** They may not have time to do this during your lessons, but if they really want to do it, there are good computer-aided learning packages for just such a purpose. Explain that if they use computers a great deal, it is perfectly possible for them to become much faster at keyboarding than they may be at handwriting.

Also explain that using the right fingers for the right letters makes keyboarding easier in the long run, even though it has to be learned in the first place.

4   **Consider the possibility of having at least one machine where plastic covers or stick-on labels obscure some or all of the letters on the keyboard.** This is one of the techniques used to help people to develop touch-typing skills. Tell pupils using such machines not to look at their fingers at all, but to watch the letters on the screen as they type. Remind them that it does not matter if they type incorrect letters; they can always delete them and try again until they manage to type it correctly on the screen.

5   **Give your pupils computer-based exercises which require them to enter words or numbers from the keyboard.** Many computer-based learning packages, and also computer-managed assessment programmes, require pupils to use text-entry and number-entry for their answers to at least some of the interactive elements.

6   **Help your pupils to become mouse-trained.** The best way for them to do this is simply to work through computer-based packages which require quite a lot of mouse-work, such as using drop-down menus, double-clicking icons, and so on. Explain that it's a bit like learning to drive a car. While there are various kinds of mouse (including roller-balls, trackpads, and various other ways of manipulating the position of the cursor on the screen), once competence has been gained using one system, different systems are relatively easy to learn.

7   **Suggest to your pupils that they may benefit from varying the sensitivity of the mouse.** When they get really competent with a mouse, they are likely to prefer using fast speeds, but using slow speeds can help them gain confidence on the way.

8   **Get pupils to experiment with the size and shape of the on-screen cursor.** The biggest source of anxiety, when learning to use a mouse, tends to be associated with 'losing' the cursor on the screen. Altering the colour and size of the cursor, to make it easier to spot, takes away much of this anxiety.

9   **Get your pupils to do some exercises using just the cursor keys on the keyboard.** These can do all the cursor movements that are normally done using a mouse, but are usually much slower and more-cumbersome. Pupils are then more likely to appreciate the benefits of being mouse-trained.

10 **Choose some exercises that develop mouse-skills.** It can be productive to get your pupils to play with a 'painting' programme, both to draw shapes and objects using the mouse, and to select and fill different areas of their drawings. People who have hang-ups about their artistic skills often find that they exceed their own expectations when trying to draw in a completely new medium.

56

Finding out how computer-assisted learning is going

The danger is that only the *computer* knows how well pupils are learning things from it during computer-assisted learning! The following suggestions may help you to keep track of your pupils' learning, and help you focus your interventions.

1 **Watch carefully as pupils start working through any new computer-assisted program.** Whenever you notice anyone who has become stuck, or who looks puzzled, find out exactly what the stumbling block was. Sometimes, you may *intend* them to become momentarily stuck, so that they work out for themselves what to do next, but at other times you may wish to adjust your briefing instructions, or the program itself, to prevent them getting stuck at such points.

2 **Use any tracking capability already built in to the computer programs.** Many computer-aided learning packages automatically track the various pathways chosen by individual users, and it can be very worthwhile to retrace individual pupils' steps from time to time, to diagnose any aspects of the program which could be causing confusion.

3 **Ask your pupils what they think of the computer-assisted packages.** However, don't just ask general questions; structure your questions to focus in on particular aspects of the packages. In particular, if you already know that a given element of the package seems to cause problems, target such elements directly in your questions.

4 **Ask pupils what they like most about the learning package.** It is useful to ask them for a given number of favourite things, two or three for example. Analyse their responses, and look for ways that you can make more use of the things that they like. When selecting new packages, keep their preferences firmly in mind.

5   **Ask directly about what they *don't* like about a package.** Sometimes there will be nothing you can do to change the package itself, but you may still be able to adjust your briefings to pupils about how best to approach using the package. When possible, however, try to adjust the software itself so that the most common grumbles are eliminated.

6   **Consider getting the computer to collect pupils' feedback for you.** It may be possible, for example, to build into the learning package intermittent multiple-choice questions about how pupils are feeling about the package at given stages, and to use the computer to store their selections of options.

7   **Sometimes, use groups of pupils to provide you with feedback.** The feedback that you can get from groups can be more valuable than from individuals, as you capture the products of group discussion. For example, ask groups to prioritize what they like best about the package, and what they like least.

8   **Don't ask questions lightly.** However pupils' feedback is being gathered, don't waste their time on questions where you don't want to (or don't need to) know the answers. For example, there's no point gathering information on people's age, gender, and so on unless you know that you intend to put to use the information that you gather. Most questionnaires can be reduced significantly without affecting their purpose.

9   **Use tests and exercises to find out how well pupils learned from computer-based packages.** When you find something that most of them learned well, try to work out what it was about the particular packages that caused such success. Conversely, if most pupils seem to have had difficulty learning something, try to find out why this was so.

10 **Give pupils feedback about their feedback!** If you're just seen to be gathering information rather than doing positive things *with* the data you collect, pupils may not be particularly willing to give you well-thought-out feedback. Show your pupils that you take their feedback seriously. Tell them what you are planning to do as a result of their feedback.

57

Using e-mail to support learning

Electronic communication is addictive! Now e-mail can be used by just about anyone with access to on-line computer networks or the Internet, and is no longer something just for technophiles. To most people who have already climbed the learning curve of finding out how to use e-mail, the apprehension they may have experienced on their first encounters fades into insignificance. E-mail can be an important medium in learning. The following suggestions may help you to maximize some of the benefits it can offer both to you and to your pupils.

1   **If you haven't already used e-mail, try to find time to learn about it yourself.** In practice, you don't need to be highly experienced with it to be ready to start sharing your expertise with your pupils. When you've just learned about it yourself, you may be in a better position to help your pupils with it, as you will still be able to remember the things you may have found difficult at first, and how to deal with them.

2   **Make sure that pupils get started with e-mail.** Write careful, step-by-step briefing instructions for your pupils. The computer-literate pupils may hardly do more than glance at these before getting into the swing of using e-mail. However, for those pupils with less confidence or experience with computers, these instructions can be vital and comforting until they become familiar with the medium.

3   **Decide what you really want to do with e-mail.** There are numerous purposes that e-mail can serve, and you need to ensure that the purpose is always clear to your pupils. If they know *what* it is being used for, and *why* e-mail has been chosen for this, they are much more likely to get more out of it.

4   **Show pupils how e-mail can be used to send much more than words.** Although you may just want to use e-mail for routine communication with (and between) pupils, there are many more uses that the medium can lend itself to. Think about the possible uses of sending attached files, such as documents, assignments, digitally-stored images, sounds and video-recordings. All of these can be edited or marked, and returned to pupils, in the same ways as simple messages.

5   **Make most messages really brief and to the point.** Few people take much notice of long e-mail messages. If something takes more than one screen, most readers either dump them or file them. Encourage your pupils also to make good use of the medium, and to send several short messages rather than try to cram lots of points into a single missive.

6   **Take particular care with your e-mail message titles.** It can take ages to search for a particular e-mail if it is not clear what each message is about. The computer software can sort messages by date, and by sender, but it is more difficult to track down topics. Two or three well-chosen keywords make the most useful titles.

7   **Make the most of the lack of time constraints.** One of the most significant advantages of e-mail as a vehicle for feedback is that pupils can view the feedback when they have time to make sense of it. They can also look at it as often as they wish to, and you can keep copies of exactly what you said to each individual pupil.

8   **Be quick to reply to your pupils!** When pupils are accustomed to e-mail, they expect quick replies to their queries. If you're going to be away from your access to the system for more than a day or two at a time, it is worth letting all your pupils know when you will be back on-line.

9   **Make the most of the speed.** If you are using e-mail to deliver to pupils your feedback comments on work you have marked, the sooner they get it, the more likely it is that their own thinking is still fresh in their minds, and the feedback is therefore better understood.

10 **Encourage pupils to reply about your feedback.** This lets you know that it has been received, but more importantly gives them the chance to let you know how they feel about the feedback you have given them, or the mark or grade that you may have awarded them.

58

Helping pupils to get started with e-mail

The use of electronic mail has accelerated rapidly in the last few years. People who would not have considered themselves computer-literate often take their first steps into the area because they are attracted by the benefits of e-mail. Some, perhaps many, of your pupils are likely to be up to speed with computers and e-mail, but the following suggestions may help you to whet the appetites of those who have not yet become 'mouse-trained'.

1   **Mention how unlikely it is that pupils will break the computer!** Some pupils may worry that they may do something drastic and irreversible to expensive equipment. Remind pupils that the only thing they are likely to risk when using computers is losing some of the work they have done with the machine, and even this risk is quite small, with 'undo' commands in most computer software, and with good habits about saving work to disk every few minutes.

2   **Point out that e-mail is a way of practising useful written com-munication skills.** Getting pupils to communicate with each other, and with you, using e-mail helps them to develop their written command of the language, including pay-off in terms of spelling and grammar. Seeing their own words on-screen rather than on paper can make them more aware of their strengths and weaknesses with the language.

3   **Promote the benefits of computer literacy.** The information technology revolution has meant that a much greater proportion of people need to use computers in their everyday work and lives. Being computer-literate also means that people don't have to rely on other people to perform various tasks for them.

4   **Remind pupils that an e-mail message need not be sent until they are completely happy with it.** This allows them to edit and polish their writing. If they were to attempt so much editing on a hand-written message, it could either look very messy, or have to be written out several times before the same amount of adjustments had been achieved.

5   **Remind pupils that e-mail can be viewed as environment-friendly.** The saving of paper can be significant. If the computing facilities are already available, it can be argued that using e-mail incurs negligible costs.

6   **Point out to pupils that they can save and keep their own e-mail communications.** By copying each e-mailed message to their own files or discs, they can keep track of all the messages they have composed and sent. Keeping similar track of handwritten messages is less likely, or would involve the trouble and expense of photocopying. Pupils looking back at a range of e-mails they have composed can see for themselves how their skills with the language are developing.

7   **Help pupils to get take that first step.** Probably the best way to do this is for you to *require* all of your pupils to e-mail something short to you, with a time deadline. It can be worth thinking about using a short written exercise for this purpose, in which case you can attach at least some marks to the task. This can make all the difference to pupils who might otherwise not get round to finding out how to log in to the system and send an e-mail.

8   **Make pupils' efforts worthwhile.** If you've asked all members of a group to e-mail something to you, try to respond *immediately* (within a day or two) to each message as it arrives. The fact that pupils get a little individual feedback via e-mail from you, and quickly, helps them to see for themselves the potential of e-mail as a communication medium.

9   **Encourage pupils to write *short* e-mails!** One of the problems with e-mail communication is that people only tend to read the beginning of a message. If an incoming message is too long for immediate reading, people tend either to file them away for later reading (and forget them!) or simply delete them.

10 **Get your pupils to select, then print out, their best e-mails.** These can be part of the evidence that goes into their portfolios of work. Getting them to pick the best ones helps to remind them of what you are trying to get them to do regarding good communication with the medium.

59

Giving pupils feedback using e-mail

E-mail is particularly useful as a vehicle for giving pupils individual feedback on assessed work, and can save you time and energy as you mark their work. E-mail feedback can extend usefully, from time to time, to giving pupils feedback on handwritten work that they have submitted for assessment. The following suggestions may help you to exploit the benefits of e-mail, not least to save you time and energy in giving pupils feedback.

1   **Make the most of the comfort of privacy.** When pupils receive feedback by e-mail (as opposed to face-to-face or in class), they have the comfort of being able to read the feedback without anyone (particularly you!) being able to see their reactions to it. This is most useful when you need to give some critical feedback to pupils.

2   **Remember that you can edit your own feedback before you send it.** For example, you may well want to adjust individual feedback comments in the light of pupils' overall performance. It is much harder to edit your own handwritten feedback on pupils' written work. E-mail allows you to type in immediate feedback to things that you see in each pupil's work, and to adjust or delete particular parts of your feedback as you go further into marking their work.

3   **Exploit the space.** Inserting handwritten feedback comments into pupils' written work is limited by the amount of space that there may be for your comments. With e-mail feedback, you don't have to restrict your wording if you need to elaborate on a point.

4   **Consider combining e-mail feedback with written feedback.** Occasionally, for example, you can write onto pupils' work a series of numbers of letters, at the points where you wish to give detailed feedback. The e-mail feedback can then translate these numbers or letters into

feedback comments or phrases, so that pupils can see exactly what each element of feedback is telling them. The fact that pupils sometimes have to decode the feedback can help them to think about it more deeply, and learn from it effectively.

5 **Spare yourself from repeated typing.** When designing computer-delivered feedback messages, you should aim towards only having to type each important message once. You can then copy and paste any of the messages when you need to give several pupils the same feedback information. It can be useful to combine this process with numbers or letters which you write onto pupils' work, and building up each e-mail to individual pupils by pasting together the feedback messages which go with each of the numbers or letters.

6 **Consider the possibilities of 'global' feedback messages.** For example, you may wish to give all of the pupils in a class the same feedback message about overall matters arising from a test or exercise. The overall message can be pasted into each e-mail, before the individual comments addressed to each pupil.

7 **Check that your e-mail feedback is getting through.** Most e-mail systems can be programmed to send you back a message saying when the e-mail was opened, and by whom. This can help you to identify any pupils who are not succeeding at opening their e-mails. It can also be useful sometimes to end each e-mail with a question asking the pupil to reply to you on some point arising from the feedback. This helps to make sure that pupils don't just open their e-mail feedback messages, but have to read them!

8 **Keep records of your e-mail feedback.** It is easy to keep copies on disk of all of your feedback to each pupil, and you can open a folder for each pupil if you wish. This makes it much easier to keep track of your on-going feedback to individual pupils, than when your handwritten feedback is lost to you when you return their work to them. If you use e-mail a lot for feedback, these collections of feedback save time when you come to writing reports.

9 **Make the most of the technology.** For example, many e-mail systems support spell-check facilities, which can allow you to type really fast and ignore most of the resulting errors, until you correct them all just before sending your message. This also causes you to re-read each message, which can be very useful for encouraging you to add second-thoughts which may have occurred to you as you went further in your assessment of the task.

10 **Use e-mail to gather feedback from your pupils.** Pupils are often bolder sitting at a computer terminal than they are face-to-face with you. Ask your pupils questions about how they are finding selected aspects of their studies, but don't turn it into an obvious routine questionnaire. Include some open-ended questions, so that they feel free to let you know how they are feeling about their own progress, and (if you're brave enough!) about your teaching too.

60

Helping pupils to learn with computer conferencing

There are several parallel names for this, including computer-mediated communication (CMC), computer-supported co-operative learning, and, more simply, on-line learning. Whatever we call them, computer conferences can be of great value in learning programmes. Many of the suggestions made about e-mail continue to apply, but in this section we would like to alert you to some of the additional factors to consider with computer conferences. You can set up computer conferences for special interest topics. Alternatively, it can be useful to set up broader conferences to serve particular identified needs of pupils across a range of groups, or across the whole school, or even in collaboration with other schools. The following suggestions may help you to maximize the benefits that your pupils can derive from computer conferencing.

1 **Note the differences between computer conferencing and other forms of electronic communication.** The distinguishing feature of computer conferencing is that many people can see the same contents, from different places, and at any time. The contents 'grow' as further notes and replies are added by participants. Most systems automatically alert participants to 'new messages' that have been added since they last viewed the conference, and allow these messages to be read first if desired.

2 **Regard computer conferences as virtual classrooms, common rooms and libraries.** They can provide a virtual classroom, where the whole pupil group can 'meet'. They can be used to provide a virtual seminar room, closed to all but a small learning group of around six pupils. They can function as virtual libraries, where resource banks and materials are kept. They can also function as pupil-only gossip areas. Each of these ways of using computer conferences can emulate electronically the related best practice in face-to-face learning environments.

3   **Get involved in computer-conferencing situations yourself first.** If you have access to e-mail or the Internet, one of the best ways to pave the way towards putting computer conferencing to good use with your pupils is to participate yourself. For example, join some discussion lists, and experience at first hand the things that work and the things that go wrong with such means of communication.

4   **Explore the computer conferencing systems from which you can choose.** If, of course, there is already a system up and running in your school, you will probably need to make the best of it anyway. If you're responsible for choosing the system, it is useful to do your research on this. There are several systems available round the world, each with their own formats, features and idiosyncrasies. If most of your pupils are not particularly computer-literate, go for a system that makes it as easy as possible to log-on and to add messages.

5   **Sell the idea to your pupils.** Explain the benefits of participating in computer conferences. Pupils can exchange a lot of information, both study-related and social, through such conferences. They can get peer-feedback on their own ideas, and even on selected parts of their work. Participating in computer conferences helps pupils to develop computer-related skills, and can quickly help them to speed up their keyboarding skills.

6   **Work out definite purposes for each computer conference.** Conferences are much more successful where they are provided to relate to identified needs, or specific intended outcomes.

7   **Make sure that all of your pupils will be able to access all the conferences which you want them to.** Ideally, you may also intend them to be able to download and/or print chosen extracts from the conference for their own personal study purposes. You can only build a computer conference into a program as an essential component if all of your pupils are able to participate. If the conference is just an optional extra for those able to join it, other pupils who can't may be able to claim to have been disadvantaged.

8   **Provide good 'start-up' pages.** These are essentially the main topics of the conference, and are listed sequentially in the main directory of the conference. Conferencing takes place when participants add 'replies' to these pages. The replies are normally listed in the sub-directory of each start-up page in the order in which they are received.

9   **Make each screen speak for itself.** Especially with 'start-up' pages, which introduce each topic in the conference, it is best that the essence of the main message takes up less than a single screen. Further detail can be added in the next few pages (or 'replies'). Encourage pupils contributing their own replies to keep them to a single screen whenever possible, and to send several replies with different titles rather than one long reply addressing a number of different aspects.

10 **Choose the titles of starter pages carefully.** When pupils are looking at the directory of a computer conference, they will see the titles of these pages arranged as an index, in the order in which the pages were originally entered. Aim to make these titles self-explanatory, so that pupils can tell what each section of the conference is about, directly from the directory, rather than having to read the whole of a starter page before finding out whether they wish to explore the topic further.

11 **Don't cover too much in a starter page.** It is better if each section of the conference is relatively self-contained, and prescribed, rather than having topic pages which cover several different aspects. As new matters arise from pupils' replies to starter pages, decide whether to introduce new starter pages to carry these matters forward separately. Add your own responses directing pupils who may be following the conference themes regarding where in the conference each theme is being developed further.

12 **Use the conference as a notice board.** Get into the habit of making the conference the best way to keep up with topical developments in the subject of study, as well as administrative matters such as assessment deadlines, guidance for pupils preparing assessments, and so on. Try to make it necessary for pupils to log-on to the conference regularly; this will result in a greater extent of active contribution by them.

13 **Use the conference as a support mechanism.** This can save a lot of your time. Elements of explanation, advice or counselling that otherwise may have had to be sent individually to several different pupils can be put into the conference once only, and remain available to all. Whenever your reply to an enquiry or problem raised by a pupil warrants a wider audience, the conference is there to do this.

14 **Make the conference a resource in its own right.** Add some screens of useful resource material, maybe with 'hot-links' to other Internet sources that are relevant. It is useful if some such material is *only* available through the computer conference; this ensures that all your pupils will make efforts to use it.

15 **Try to get pupils discussing and arguing with each other via the conference.** The best computer conferences are not just teacher–pupil debates, but are taken over by the pupils themselves. They can add new topics, and bring a social dimension to the conference.

16 **Consider having some assessed work entered onto the conference.** If pupils *have to* make some contributions, they are more likely to ascend the learning curve regarding sending in replies, and to do so more readily in non-assessed elements too. One advantage in having an assessed task 'up on the conference' is that each pupil can see everyone else's attempts, and the standards of work improve very rapidly.

17 **Moderate computer conferences rigorously.** For example, remove anything offensive or inappropriate before it is likely to be seen by many pupils. If particular pupils mis-use the conference, treat the issue seriously, and seek them out and warn them of the consequences of such actions, for example loss of computer privileges. It is useful to recruit pupil moderators from those pupils who are particularly computer-literate, and who may be only too willing to become conference moderators, editing and re-arranging contributions to keep the structure of the conference fluent and easy to follow.

61

Using video for learning

Video recordings are widely used in many forms of teaching and learning, and already play a valuable role in helping to show pupils things that they would not be in a position to explore on their own. However, the act of watching material on a television screen is not one of the most powerful ways through which pupils actually learn, unless the video extracts are carefully planned into their learning programme. The following suggestions may help you help your pupils to make the most of video.

1   **Decide whether the video is just for fun.** It is perfectly legitimate to decide that a particular video showing will just be intended as a 'sit back and watch this' occasion, and that pupils will be expected to do no more than enjoy the experience. If this is the case, tell your pupils so. However, such occasions are a luxury, and it is important to tell pupils whether or not a video is an integral part of something that they are learning. The remaining suggestions in this section aim to help you make best use of those videos that are not just for fun.

2   **Decide what the intended learning outcomes directly associated with the video extracts will be.** It is important that any video extracts are not just seen as an optional extra by your pupils. The best way to prevent this from happening is to tell them exactly what they are intended to gain from each extract of video material.

3   **Decide why video is the best medium for your purposes.** Ask yourself 'what is this video extract doing that could not be done just in print?'. Video extracts can be invaluable for showing all sorts of things that pupils could not experience directly, as well as for conveying all of the subtleties that go with body language, facial expression, tone of voice, and interpersonal interactions, skills and techniques.

4   **Decide how the video material is planned to help your pupils to learn.** Is it primarily intended to whet their appetites and stimulate their motivation? Is it designed to help them to make sense of some important ideas or concepts which are hard to learn without seeing things? Is it designed to give them useful briefings about things they themselves are intended to do after watching the material?

5   **Consider whether your pupils could need their own copies of the video.** If they are intended to watch the video a number of times, and at their own choices of points during their learning, you may need to issue them with personal copies, or make them available on loan. Alternatively, you may be able to arrange that the materials can be viewed on demand in a resources centre. If so, make sure that there are mechanisms enabling pupils to book a time-slot when they can see the video material.

6   **Decide what your pupils will take away after watching the video.** One of the dangers with video extracts is the 'now you see it, then it's gone' situation. If the video is serving important purposes for your pupils, they will need to have something more permanent to remind them of what they learned from it. Since, even if they have their own copies of the video material, they are unlikely to find time to revise from it directly, it is important that they have some other kind of summary of what they are expected to remember from it.

7   **Work out what (if anything) will be assessed.** If the video is just 'icing on the cake' and there is nothing arising from the video material that will be directly involved in any form of assessment, tell your pupils that this is the case. When things they derive from using the video elements *are* involved in their assessment, explain this to them, to help them give the video materials appropriate attention.

8   **Use short extracts at a time.** People are conditioned to watch quite long episodes of television, but to do so in a relatively passive way. Make sure that your pupils approach video extracts in a different way than that which they normally use for watching television. It is better to split up a 30-minute video into half a dozen or so separate episodes if there are several different things you wish your pupils to get out of the material. Some video materials have timings encoded onto the video tape.

9   **Set the agenda for your pupils *before* each episode of video.** This can be done by you before showing each of the video extracts themselves, or can be done through accompanying handout materials. Either way, ensure that your pupils are set up with questions in their minds, to which the video extracts will provide answers.

10 **Consider giving your pupils things to do** *while* **they view the video extracts.** You could brief them to note down particular observations, or to make particular decisions, or to extract and record specific facts or figures as they watch the video episodes.

11 **Consider asking your pupils to do things** *after* **they've watched each extract.** This can help them to consolidate what they have gained from watching the extracts. It can also prompt them to try to have a further look, if this is possible, at any extract where they may have slipped into passive viewing mode and missed important points.

12 **Don't underestimate the importance of handout support materials.** To make the most of video elements, pupils need something in another medium to remind them about what they should be getting out of the video, and where it fits into the overall picture of their learning. Video recordings often work best when supported by a task-sheet or workbook, into which pupils write their observations and their interpretations of what they see. Their learning from such handouts can be reviewed by looking again at them, even without looking again at the recording.

62

Using audiotapes for learning

Audiotape is so commonplace and cheap that its potential in learning contexts is easily overlooked. In subject disciplines such as music, where sound is all-important, the use of audiotapes as a learning medium is already well developed. In multimedia packages, sound and images are often combined to good effect, yet audiotape can sometimes play a similar role at much less cost. The use of audiotapes to support learning can be extended to many disciplines. The following suggestions may help you to put audiotape to good use to support your pupils.

1   **Have good reasons for using audiotapes.** Always be in a position to explain to your pupils why an audiotape is being used alongside their other learning resource materials. Share with them information on what they should be getting out of using the audiotape.

2   **Most pupils have access to audiotape.** Many pupils have portable cassette players, and may use these when travelling on public transport, or jogging, and in all sorts of circumstances. When elements of learning packages are available as audiotapes, there is the possibility that you will extend their learning to times when they would not otherwise be attempting to study.

3   **Label audiotapes informatively.** People who listen to tapes tend to accumulate lots of them, and it is easy for audiocassettes accompanying learning programmes to get lost amid those used for entertainment.

4   **Disable re-recording.** Remove the tags from the back of each audiotape, so that pupils can't accidentally record over the material on the tape. They can still do so deliberately of course, by placing adhesive tape over the tab positions! Always keep several back-up copies of audiotape materials that you issue to pupils, and don't expect to get all of your issued copies back intact!

5   **Keep audiotape extracts short and sharp, and link them to handout materials.** When there are specific intentions about what pupils should get out of listening to audiotapes, extracts should normally last for a few minutes rather than quarters of an hour! It is worth starting each extract with a recorded 'name' such as 'Extract 3, to go with Section 1, Part 2', and to have the same voice reminding pupils that when they have reached the 'End of extract 3, going with Section 1, Part 2', and so on.

6   **Use audiotape where tone of voice is important.** It can be particularly useful for pupils to hear messages, where the emphasis that you place on key words or phrases helps them to make sense of material which would be harder to interpret from a printed page or from a computer screen.

7   **Sound can help pupils into subject-related jargon.** When there is new terminology, for example, it can be hard to tell how to pronounce a word just by seeing it in print, and it can be humiliating for pupils to find only when talking to a teacher that they have got their pronunciation wrong! Audiotapes can introduce the vocabulary of a subject to pupils. It goes without saying that audiotapes come into their own when helping pupils to learn the pronunciation of languages.

8   **Use audiotapes to bring learning to life.** Audiotapes can be invaluable for giving pupils the chance to hear people talking, discussing, debating, arguing, persuading, counselling, criticizing, and can capture and pass on to them many experiences and processes which would be difficult to capture in print.

9   **Clarify exactly when a recorded episode should be used.** If you are using audiotape alongside printed materials, it can be useful to have a visual 'flag' to indicate to your pupils when they should listen to a recorded extract.

10 **Turn pupils' listening into an active process.** Listening can all too easily be a passive process. Avoid this by setting your pupils things to think about before listening to a tape extract. Prime them with a few questions, so that they will be searching for the answers from what they hear.

11 **Consider using audiotape to give pupils feedback on their assignments.** It can be quicker to talk for a few minutes into a tape recorder, than to write all of your feedback down on your pupils' written assignments. The added intimacy of tone of voice can help you to deliver critical feedback in a more acceptable form. Besides, pupils may regard it as something special to have such a distinguished voice talking directly to them! Pupils can also play the tape again and again, until they have

understood each part of your recorded feedback. Always try to begin and end with something positive, just as you would do with written feedback.

12 **Combine audio and visual learning.** For example, it can be useful to use audiotape to talk pupils through things that they are looking at in their resource materials. For example, complex diagrams or derivations in printed materials, or graphics, tables, spreadsheets shown on-screen in computer-based materials, can be brought to life by the sound of a human voice explaining what to look for in them.

63

Using multimedia packages for learning

Learning packages can contain, or refer to, an increasing range of other kinds of material. We explored the use of videotapes in a separate set of suggestions, but the present set aims to alert you to the questions you should be asking yourself about any medium. This could range from CD-ROMs, the Internet, intranets, interactive videos, and anything which adds sounds, still pictures, moving images, graphics, to the experience of pupils working through learning materials.

1   **How does the medium help pupils' motivation?** Ideally, any multimedia component should help pupils to want to learn from them. If there are too many steps to getting going with the multimedia elements, there is the danger that pupils can be put off, and maybe stopped in their tracks.

2   **Can the medium be used to provide some learning-by-doing?** Perhaps the biggest danger with some multimedia packages is that, however sophisticated the media used, pupils may only be spectators rather than players. Where it is not possible to cause pupils to interact directly with the materials, it remains possible to get them to make decisions, answer questions, and summarize conclusions, and to write down these for later reference.

3   **Can the medium be used to give pupils feedback?** The danger is that the information presented using multimedia is often fixed, and cannot then respond to what pupils may be thinking about it, or to the problems or misunderstandings that may be in their minds. Multimedia materials which *respond* to pupils immediately after they have done something are better at helping to make pupils' learning effective as well as enjoyable.

4   **How does the medium help pupils to make sense of things?** There are often excellent answers to this question. For example, sounds, pictures, moving images, and colourful graphics can all play useful parts in helping pupils to get their heads round things with which they have been grappling.

5   **Why is this medium better than other, cheaper media?** For example, why is a computer-based package better than a print-based one? There are many good answers to this question. The best answers are when the medium chosen does something that just cannot be done by other media, for example, moving pictures showing body language and facial expression where such dimensions are crucially important for getting particular messages or attitudes across to pupils.

6   **How relevant will the medium-based element be to the overall learning programme?** One of the dangers with media-based learning is that too much 'nice-to-know' material may be involved, and not enough emphasis placed on 'need-to-know' material, and that pupils may not easily be able to distinguish the two categories.

7   **How will the choice of medium affect pupils' opportunities to learn?** For example, will they only be able to study the particular elements concerned when they are sitting at a networked computer terminal, or when logged on to the Internet? Will this mean that they have frequently to stop learning until they can gain such access? Will there be alternative coverage of these elements of learning for any pupils who have not got easy access to the medium, and can it be guaranteed that they will not end up disadvantaged?

8   **How easy will it be to edit and change the medium-based elements?** Learning materials are never 'finished'. There are always adjustments and changes that are indicated from piloting, feedback from pupils, and from assessments measuring how well pupils actually succeeded in their learning. Some media are much easier to edit and change than others. Changing a CD-ROM or videodisk is a much more complex (and more expensive) business than changing a file in a computer-based package.

9   **What other media could have been used?** There is rarely just one way to package a particular element of learning. It is useful to explore at least two or three alternative ways of using media to deliver each element of learning, and then to make an informed decision about why a particular medium is chosen.

10 **How will pupils revise and consolidate what they have learned from the medium?** What will they have to take away? Will they be able to make a structured summary of what they learned while working with the medium, which will bring all the important points back to their minds when looking at it later?

64

Using the Internet for learning

Pupils may be able to use the Internet at times of their own choice, in their own ways, at their own pace, and from anywhere in school or beyond, where access to it is available to them. That said, this does not mean that it is automatically a vehicle for productive and effective learning. Indeed, it is very easy to become side-tracked by all sorts of fascinating things, and to stray well away from any intended learning outcome. The suggestions which follow are not intended as starting points for setting out to *deliver* learning through the Internet, but rather to help pupils to *use* the Internet to obtain material in connection with their studies, such as in assignments they are preparing. The following suggestions may help you to help your pupils both to enjoy the Internet, and to learn well from it.

1   **Play with the Internet yourself.** You need to pick up your own experience of how it feels to tap into such a vast and varied database, before you can design ways of using it to offer your pupils some meaningful learning experiences.

2   **Decide whether you want your pupils to use the Internet, or an Intranet.** An Intranet is where a networked set of computers talk to each other, whilst using Internet conventions, but where the content is not open to the rest of the universe. If you are working in a school which already has such a network, and if your pupils can make use of this network effectively, there will be some purposes that will be better served by an Intranet. You can also have *controlled* access to the Internet via an Intranet, such as by using hot-links to pre-determined external sites.

3   **Use the Internet to research something yourself.** You may well of course have done this often already, but if not, give it a try before you think of setting your pupils 'search and retrieve' tasks with the Internet. Set yourself a fixed time, perhaps half-an-hour or even less. Choose a topic that you're going to search for, preferably something a little offbeat. See

for yourself how best to use the search engines, and compare the efficiency of different engines. Find out for yourself how to deal with 4,593 references to your chosen topic, and how to improve your searching strategy to whittle them down to the ten that you really want to use!

4   **Don't just use the Internet as a filing cabinet for your own learning resources!** While it is useful in its own way if your pupils can have access to your own notes and resources, this is not really *using* the Internet. Too many materials designed for use in other forms are already cluttering up the Internet. If all you intend your pupils to do is to download your notes and print their own copies, sending them e-mailed attachments would do the same job much more efficiently.

5   **Think carefully about your intended learning outcomes.** You may indeed wish to use the Internet as a means whereby your pupils address the existing intended outcomes associated with their subject material. However, it is also worth considering whether you may wish to add further learning outcomes, to do with the processes of searching, selecting, retrieving, and analysing subject material. If so, you may also need to think about whether, and how, these additional learning outcomes may be assessed.

6   **Give your pupils specific things to do using the Internet.** Make these tasks where it is relevant to have up-to-the-minute data or news, rather than where the 'answers' are already encapsulated in easily accessible books or learning resources.

7   **Consider giving your pupils a menu of tasks and activities.** They will feel more ownership if they have a significant degree of choice in their Internet tasks. Where you have a group of pupils working on the same syllabus, it can be worth letting them choose different tasks, and then communicating their main findings to each other (and to you) using a computer conference or by e-mail.

8   **Let your pupils know that the process is at least as important as the outcome.** The key skills that they can develop using the Internet include designing an effective search, and making decisions about the quality and authenticity of the evidence they find. It is worth designing tasks where you already know of at least some of the evidence you expect them to locate, and remaining open to the fact that they will each uncover at least as much again as you already know about!

9   **Consider designing your own interactive pages.** You may want to restrict these to an Intranet, at least at first. You can then use dialogue boxes to make your pupils answer questions, enter data, and so on. Putting such pages up for all to see on the Internet may mean that you get a lot of unsolicited replies!

10   **Consider getting your pupils to design and enter some pages.** This may be best done restricted to an Intranet, at least until your pupils have picked up sufficient skills to develop pages that are worth putting up for all to see. The act of designing their own Internet material is one of the most productive ways to help your pupils develop their critical skills at evaluating materials already on the Internet.

65

Helping pupils to learn from the Internet

The Internet is the electronic highway to the largest collection of information, data and communication ever constructed by the human species. There is information available through the World Wide Web on every imaginable subject. Playing with the Internet is easy, but *learning* from it is not always straightforward. The following suggestions may help you to point your pupils in directions where they will not only enjoy playing with the Internet, but also develop their techniques so that they learn effectively from it too.

1   **Consider starting small.** For example, you might be able to download selected information from the Internet onto individual computers, or a locally networked series of terminals. You can then give your pupils specific 'search' tasks, where it will be relatively easy for them to locate specific information.

2   **Get your pupils to induct each other.** Learning from the Internet need not be a solo activity. Indeed, it can be very useful to have two or three pupils working at each terminal, so that they talk to each other about what they are finding, and follow up leads together. Encourage them to take turns at working the keyboard, so that they all develop their confidence at handling the medium, and are then equipped to carry on working on their own.

3   **Help your pupils master the use of search engines.** There are many free search engines available on the Internet. Some are faster than others, and some are more successful than others for tracking down particular fields of information. Give your pupils some exercises to help them find out which search engines suit them best.

4   **Give your pupils exercises that help them to improve their selection of search words.** Show them how choosing a single broad search word leads to far too many sources being listed, and make it very slow and boring to go through all of the sources looking for the information they are really wanting. Get them to experiment with different combinations of search words, so that the sources that are located become much more relevant to their search purposes.

5   **Allow your pupils to find out about the different speeds at which information can be found on the Internet.** For example, let them experiment at different times of the day, so they can see when the Internet is heavily used and slower. Also let them find out for themselves how much slower it can be waiting for graphics to be downloaded than for mainly text materials. Help them to become better at deciding whether to persist with a source that is highly relevant but slow to download, or whether to continue searching for sources which may download more quickly.

6   **Remind your pupils that finding information is only the first step in learning from it.** It is only too easy to discover a wealth of information during an Internet search, only to forget most of it within a very short time.

7   **Help your pupils to learn to keep tabs on what they have found.** Entering 'bookmarks' or 'favourites' is one of the most efficient ways of being able to go back easily to what may have turned out to be the most relevant or valuable source of information during a search. Get your pupils to practise logging the sites that could turn out to be worth returning to. Also help them to practise clearing out bookmarks that turn out to be irrelevant, or that are superseded by later finds.

8   **Give your pupils practice at recording things that they have found during searches.** It can be useful to design worksheets to train them to note down key items of information as they find it, and to teach them to be better at making their own notes as a matter of routine when exploring a topic using the Internet.

9   **Help your pupils to develop their critical skills.** The authenticity and validity of information found using the Internet vary enormously. It is not possible to tell whether information is good or bad just by looking at the apparent quality of it on the screen. Remind your pupils that information on the Internet may not have been subjected to refereeing or other quality-assurance processes normally associated with published information in books or journal articles.

10 **Remind pupils to balance playing with the Internet and learning from it.** It is perfectly natural, and healthy, to explore, and to follow up interesting leads, even when they take pupils far away from the purpose of their searches. However, it is useful to develop the skills to ration the amount of random exploration, and to devote 'spurts' of conscious activity to following through the specific purposes of searches.

Postscript

We hope that these suggestions will be useful to you in your teaching career. You may well feel that your experiences put you in a position where you too have advice to give to other teachers. If so, we will be delighted to hear from you, and may well (with your permission) include your ideas, properly credited, in the next edition of this volume.

Further reading

Alcott, M (1997) *Introduction to Children with Special Educational Needs* Hodder and Stoughton, London.

Anderson, D, Brown, S and Race, P (1998) *500 Tips for Further and Continuing Education Lecturers* Kogan Page, London.

Baumann, A S, Broomfield, A and Roughton, L (1997) *Becoming a Secondary School Teacher* Hodder and Stoughton, London.

Bradley, H (1991) *Staff Development* School Development and Management of Change Series, Falmer Press, London.

Haines, C (1996) *School Improvement – Practical Strategies to Enhance Teaching and Learning* Folems, London.

Hayes, D (1997) *Success on your Teaching Experience* Hodder and Stoughton, London.

Hopkins, D, Ainscow, M and West, M (1994) *School Development in an Era of Change* School Development Series, Cassell, London.

Horne, H and Brown, S (1997) *500 Tips for School Improvement* Kogan Page, London.

Horne, H and Pierce, A (1996) *A Practical Guide to Staff Development and Appraisal in Schools* Kogan Page, London.

Horne, H (ed.) (1998) *The School Management Handbook* (5th edition) Kogan Page, London.

Kyriacou, C (1991) *Essential Teaching Skills* Blackwell, Oxford.

OFSTED/DfEE (1996) *Setting Targets to Improve Standards* HMSO, London.

Packard, E, Packard, N and Brown, S (1998) *500 Tips for Primary Teachers* Kogan Page, London.

Race, P and McDowell, S (1996) *500 Computing Tips for Lecturers and Teachers* Kogan Page, London.

Sutton, R (1994) *Assessment; A Framework for Teachers* Routledge, London.

Vahid, B, Harwood, S and Brown, S (1998) *500 Tips for Working with Children with Special Needs* Kogan Page, London.

Index

500 Tips from Kogan Page